Fairness and Efficiency in the Flat Tax

Fairness and Efficiency in the Flat Tax

Robert E. Hall, Alvin Rabushka,
Dick Armey, Robert Eisner, and
Herbert Stein

THE AEI PRESS

Publisher for the American Enterprise Institute

WASHINGTON, D.C.

1996

Available in the United States from the AEI Press, c/o Publisher Resources Inc., 1224 Heil Quaker Blvd., P.O. Box 7001, La Vergne, TN 37086-7001. Distributed outside the United States by arrangement with Eurospan, 3 Henrietta Street, London WC2E 8LU England.

Library of Congress Cataloging-in-Publication Data

Fairness and efficiency in the flat tax / Robert E. Hall . . . [et al.].
    p. cm.
  Includes bibliographical references.
  ISBN 0-8447-3986-3 (cloth : alk. paper). — ISBN 0-8447-3987-1 (pbk. : alk. paper)
    1. Flat-rate income tax—United States. 2. Income tax—United States.   I. Hall, Robert Ernest, 1943– .
HJ4652.F18   1996
336.24—dc20   96-15991
                                          CIP

1 3 5 7 9 10 8 6 4 2

The AEI PRESS
Publisher for the American Enterprise Institute
1150 17th Street, N.W., Washington, D.C. 20036

Printed in the United States of America

Contents

1
Introduction

Christopher DeMuth

The flat tax is a paradox. In one sense, it is stunningly simple—the individual's tax return on a postcard, that of General Motors on eight or nine lines.

But in another sense—its effect on incentives, investment, and the economy—it is very subtle, not to say complex. While the tax is very easy to *visualize*, it is not altogether simple to *understand*.

The purpose of this book is to explore the subtleties and ramifications, and enhance the understanding, of this proposal for sweeping tax reform. With the exception of Congressman Richard Armey, who himself is a former professor of economics, all of the authors of the chapters are well-known academic experts in taxation, including Robert Hall and Alvin Rabushka, who first proposed the flat tax more than ten years ago. These authors bring to bear an understanding of the implications of the flat tax that is not available elsewhere.

The reader will learn that the authors disagree on important points. But their analyses of the flat tax shed much needed light on an issue that has tended to become oversimplified, and even vulgarized, in political debate. Their reasoning can be readily followed by the interested but nonexpert reader, who will learn of the subtleties of this intriguing proposal.

We have all heard about the feature of the flat tax that would end the deduction for mortgage interest, for example, though the effect of this change is not at all what it seems on the surface. But what about the end of the employers' deduction for the payment of fringe benefits, leaving a deduction only for wages? And how about the provision allowing a business to take a deduction for the entire cost of a new factory in the year it is built? These have enormous implications for the efficiency of the economic system as a whole, and they are not well understood, or even known, by the public at large.

A flat tax rate is not the only, or even the most important, feature of the flat tax. Its business tax is at least as revolutionary as the individual wage tax, if not more so. Its treatment of investment, savings, and the returns from savings is wholly different from the system we now have.

Understanding the flat tax and its implications is an adventure as rewarding as any endeavor of its kind. And one day—who knows?—the flat tax may become the law of the land.

2

Putting the Flat Tax into Action

Robert E. Hall and Alvin Rabushka

Tax forms can fit on postcards. A cleanly designed tax system takes only a few elementary calculations, in contrast to the hopeless complexity of today's income taxes. We have developed a complete plan for a whole new tax system. Our system would put a low tax rate on a comprehensive definition of income. Because the tax would be applied to a wider definition of income, the tax rate would be an astonishingly low 19 percent but would raise the same revenue as does the current tax system. The proposed tax is fair to families—the poor would pay no tax at all. The tax would also be progressive: the fraction of income that a family would pay in taxes would rise with income. The proposed system is simple and easy to understand. And the tax would operate on the consumption-tax principle: families would be taxed on what they take out of the economy, not on what they put into it.

Our system rests on the basic administrative principle that income should be taxed exactly once, as close as possible to its source. Today's tax system violates this principle in all kinds of ways. Some kinds of income—such as fringe benefits—are never taxed at all. Other kinds, such as dividends and capital gains, are taxed twice. And interest income, which is supposed to be taxed once, escapes taxation completely in all too many cases, where taxpayers arrange to receive interest beyond the reach of the Internal Revenue Service.

Our plan combines the merits of an income tax and a consumption tax. The tax on wages and salaries is a pro-

3

gressive tax because—thanks to a generous initial family allowance—the proportion of income paid in taxes rises with income, even though the tax *rate* is flat. Up to an exemption level—$25,500 for a family of four—wages are untaxed. All wages above the exemption level are taxed at the same rate of 19 percent. Uniformity of the tax rate above the exemption level is a basic concept of the flat tax. Its logic is much more profound than just the simplicity of calculation with a single tax rate. Whenever different forms of consumption or income are taxed at different rates or different taxpayers face different rates, the public can take advantage of the differentials.

Progressivity, Efficiency, and Simplicity

Limiting the burden of taxes on the poor is a central principle of tax reform. Some ideas for tax simplification and reform flout this principle. Neither a federal sales tax nor a value-added tax would be progressive. Instead, all citizens, rich and poor alike, would pay essentially the same fraction of their spending in taxes. Although sales and value-added taxes generally are a form of consumption tax, we reject them for their lack of progressivity. The current federal tax system avoids taxing the poor, and we think it should stay that way.

Exempting the poor from taxes does not require graduated tax rates rising to high levels for upper-income taxpayers. A flat rate, applied to all income above a generous personal allowance, would provide progressivity without creating important differences in tax rates. Graduated taxes automatically create differences in tax rates among taxpayers, with all the attendant opportunities for leakage. Because high-income taxpayers have the biggest incentive and the best opportunity to use special tricks to exploit tax-rate differentials, applying the same tax rate to these taxpayers for all their income in all years is the most important goal of flat-rate taxation.

Our proposal is based squarely on the principle of consumption taxation. To make consumption the base upon which the tax is calculated, we use the tested principle of taxing value added with a deduction for investment spending and family allowances to ensure progressivity. The effect of our proposed tax is the same as a tax on retail sales of consumption goods but, with personal deductions added, avoids some serious administrative problems that plague sales taxes. By contrast, the tax system in the United States today taxes income—the sum of consumption and investment—with an incredible hodgepodge of provisions to encourage some types of investment and some types of saving. The total effect of these incentives is spotty. There are excessive incentives for some saving and investment channels and inadequate incentives for others. In our system, there would be a single, coherent approach based on the value-added principle to create a clean consumption tax.[1]

We believe that the simplicity of our system is a central feature. Complex tax forms and tax laws do more harm that just deforesting America. Complicated taxes require expensive advisers for taxpayers and equally expensive reviews and audits by the government. A complex tax invites the taxpayer to search for a special feature to exploit to the disadvantage of the rest of us. And complex taxes diminish confidence in government, inviting a breakdown in cooperation with the tax system and the spread of outright evasion.

An Integrated Flat Tax

Our flat tax would apply to both businesses and individuals. Although our system would have two separate tax forms—one for business income and the other for wages and salaries—it would be an integrated system. When we speak of its virtues, such as its equal tax rate for all types of income, we mean the system, not one of its two parts. As we will explain, the business tax would not just be a replacement for the existing corporate income tax. The business tax would cover all businesses, not just corporations.

5

And it would cover interest income, including that which is currently taxed as personal income.

In our system, all income would be classified as either business income or wages (including salaries and retirement benefits). The system would be airtight. Taxes on both types of income would be equal. The wage tax would have features to make the entire system progressive. Both taxes would have postcard forms. The low tax rate of 19 percent would be enough to match the revenue of the federal tax system as it existed in 1993.

Here is the logic of our system, stripped to basics: We want to tax consumption. Families do one of two things with income—spend it or invest it. We can measure consumption as income minus investment. A really simple tax would just have each firm pay tax on the total amount of income generated by the firm less that firm's investment in plant and equipment, similar to the value-added tax. But the value-added tax is unfair because it is not progressive. That is why we break the tax in two. The firm would pay tax on all the income generated at the firm except the income paid to its workers, purchases of inputs, and purchases of plant and equipment. The workers themselves would pay tax on what they earn, and the tax they pay would be progressive.

To measure the total amount of income generated at a business, we take the total receipts of the firm over the year and subtract the payments the firm has made to its workers and suppliers. This approach guarantees a comprehensive tax base. Value-added taxes in Europe work just this way. The base for the business tax is the following:

> total revenue from sales of goods and services
> *less*
> purchases of inputs from other firms
> *less*
> wages, salaries, and pensions paid to workers
> *less*
> purchases of plant and equipment

TABLE 2–1
FLAT-TAX REVENUES COMPARED WITH CURRENT REVENUES
(billions of dollars)

Line	Income or Revenue	Dollars
1	Gross domestic product	6,374
2	Indirect business tax	431
3	Income included in GDP but not in tax base	217
4	Wages, salaries, and pensions	3,100
5	Investment	723
6	Business-tax base (line 1 minus lines 2 through 5)	1,903
7	Business-tax revenue (19 percent of line 6)	362
8	Family allowances	1,705
9	Wage-tax base (line 4 less line 8)	1,395
10	Wage-tax revenue (19 percent of line 9)	265
11	Total flat-tax revenue (line 7 plus line 10)	627
12	Actual personal income tax	510
13	Actual corporate income tax	118
14	Total actual revenue (line 12 plus line 13)	627

SOURCE: U.S. National Income and Product Accounts, 1993, and authors' calculations.

The other piece is the wage tax. Each family would pay 19 percent of its wages, salary, and pension income over a family allowance. The allowance makes the system progressive. The base for the compensation tax would be total wages, salaries, and retirement benefits less the total amount of family allowances.

Table 2–1 shows how we calculate potential flat-tax revenue from the U.S. National Income and Product Accounts for 1993. The first line shows gross domestic product (GDP), the most comprehensive measure of income throughout the economy. The next two lines are items that are included in GDP but would not be taxed under the flat tax, such as sales and excise taxes. Line 3, income included in GDP but not in the tax base, is mostly the value of the services of houses owned and lived in by families; this income does not go through the market. Wages, salaries, and pensions, line 4, would be reported by the firm's workers on their wage-tax forms and would be deducted by businesses. Investment, line 5, is the amount spent by businesses on purchases of new plant and equipment (each business could also deduct its purchases of used plant and equipment, but these would be included in the taxable income of the selling business and would net out in the aggregate). Line 6 shows the potential taxable income under a flat tax of all businesses after they have deducted their wages and investment. The potential revenue from the business tax, line 7, is 19 percent of the tax base on line 6. Line 8 shows the amount of family allowances that would be deducted. The wage-tax base on line 9 shows the amount of wages, salaries, and pensions left after deducting all family allowances from the amount on line 4. The potential wage-tax revenue on line 10 is 19 percent of the base. Total flat-tax revenue on line 11 would be $627 billion. Lines 12 and 13 show the actual revenue from the personal and corporate income tax. The total actual revenue on line 14 is also $627 billion. The potential flat-tax revenue and the actual revenue are the same, by design. Our proposal is to reproduce the revenue of the actual income tax system, not to raise or to lower it.

These computations show that in 1993 the revenue from the corporate income tax, with a tax rate of 34 percent, was $118 billion. The revenue from our business tax at a rate of only 19 percent would have been $362 billion, just over three times as much, even though the tax rate is not much over half the current corporate rate. There are three main reasons that the flat business tax would yield more revenue than the existing corporate tax does. First, slightly more than half of business income is earned by noncorporate businesses—professional partnerships, proprietorships, and the like. Second, the business tax would put a tax on fringe benefits, which escape taxation in the current system, by not allowing them to be deducted. Third, by refusing to allow interest expense as a deduction, the business tax imposes tax on interest at its source in business, rather than at its destination.

The other side of the coin, of course, is that our wage tax would have yielded less revenue than the current personal income tax does—$265 billion in 1993 as against $510 billion. We are not proposing a massive shift in taxes from wages to capital income. Our wage tax would apply just to wages, salaries, and private pensions, whereas today's personal income tax includes unincorporated business income, dividends, interest, rent, and many other kinds of income that we would tax as part of business income. The switch to the more reliable principle of taxing business income at the source, rather than hoping to catch the income at the destination, is the main reason that the business tax would yield so much more revenue than the current corporate tax does.

The Individual Wage Tax. The individual wage tax would have a single purpose: to tax the large fraction of total income that employers pay as cash to their workers. It would not be a tax system by itself but would be one of the two major parts of the complete system. The base of the proposed tax is defined narrowly and precisely as actual payments of wages, salaries, and pensions. Pension contributions (as opposed to benefits) and other fringe benefits paid by employers would not be counted as part of wages. In other words, the tax on pension income would be paid when the retired worker actually receives the pension, not when the employer sets aside the money to pay the future pension. Pension contributions would not be taxed if the employer pays into a completely separate pension fund, if the worker makes a voluntary contribution to a 401(k) program, or if the worker contributes to a Keogh or other individual retirement fund. The contributions would not be taxed until they were distributed at retirement.

The tax form for our wage tax is self-explanatory. To make the tax system progressive, only earnings over a personal or family allowance would be taxed. The allowance would be $25,500 for a family of four in 1996 but would rise along with the cost of living in later years. All the taxpayer would do is report total wages, salaries, and pensions at the top of the form, compute the family allowance based on marital status and number of dependents, subtract the allowance, multiply by 19 percent to compute the tax, take account of withholding, and pay the difference or apply for a refund. For about 80 percent of the population, filling out this postcard once a year would be the only effort needed to satisfy the Internal Revenue Service. What a change from the many pages of schedules the typical frustrated taxpayer fills out today!

For the 80 percent of taxpayers who do not run businesses, the individual wage tax would be the only tax to worry about. Many features of current taxes would disappear, including charitable deductions, mortgage interest deductions, capital gains taxes, dividend taxes, and interest taxes. We will discuss these in detail later.

Anyone who is self-employed or pays expenses directly in connection with making a living would need to file the business tax to get the proper deduction for expenses. Fortunately, the business-tax form would be even simpler than the wage-tax form (see figure 2–1).

The Business Tax. It would not be the purpose of the business tax to tax businesses. Fundamentally, people pay taxes, not businesses. The idea of the business tax would be to collect the tax that the owners of a business owe on the income produced by the business. Collecting business income tax at the source of the income would avoid one of the biggest causes of leakage in the tax system today: interest can pass through many layers where it is invariably deducted when it is paid out but not so frequently reported as income.

Airtight taxation of individual business income at source is possible because we already know the tax rate of

FIGURE 2–1

Form 1	Individual Wage Tax	1996
Your first name and initial (if joint return, also give spouse's name and initial) Last name		Your social security number
Home address (number and street including apartment number or rural route)		Spouse's social security number
City, town, or post office, state, and ZIP code		Your occupation
		Spouse's occupation

1	Wages and salary	1
2	Pension and retirement benefits	2
3	Total compensation (*line 1 plus line 2*)	3
4	Personal allowance	
	(a) $16,500 for married filing jointly	4a
	(b) $9,500 for single	4b
	(c) $14,000 for single head of household	4c
5	Number of dependents, not including spouse	5
6	Personal allowances for dependents (*line 5 multiplied by $4,500*)	6
7	Total personal allowances (*line 4 plus line 6*)	7
8	Taxable compensation (*line 3 less line 7, if positive; otherwise zero*)	8
9	Tax (*19% of line 8*)	9
10	Tax withheld by employer	10
11	Tax due (*line 9 less line 10, if positive*)	11
12	Refund due (*line 10 less line 9, if positive*)	12

all the owners of the business: it is the common flat rate paid by all taxpayers. If the tax system has graduated rates, taxation at the source would become a problem. If each owner were to be taxed at that owner's rate, the business would have to find out the tax rate applicable to each owner and apply that rate to the income produced in the business for that owner. But this is only the beginning of the problem. The IRS would have to audit a business and its owners together to see that the owners were reporting the correct tax rates to the business. Further, suppose one of the owners made a mistake and was later discovered to be in a higher tax bracket. Then the business would have to refile its tax form to collect the right tax. Obviously, this system would not work. Business taxes have to be collected at the destination, from the owners, if graduated rates are to be applied. Source taxation is practical only when a single rate is applied to all owners. Because source taxation is so much more reliable and inexpensive than the present method, there is a powerful practical argument for using a single flat rate for all business income.

The business tax would be a giant, comprehensive withholding tax on all types of income other than wages, salaries, and pensions. It would be carefully designed to tax every bit of income outside of wages but to tax it only once. The business tax would not have deductions for interest payments, dividends, or any other type of payment to the owners of the business. As a result, all income that people would receive from business activity would already have been taxed. Because the tax would already have been paid, the tax system would not need to consider what would happen to interest, dividends, or capital gains after these types of income leave the firm. The resulting simplification and improvement in the tax system would be enormous. Today, the IRS receives over a billion Form 1099s, which keep track of interest and dividends, and the agency must make an overwhelming effort to match these forms to the 1040s filed by the recipients. The only reason for a Form 1099 is to track income as it makes its way from the business where it originates to the ultimate recipient. Not a single Form 1099 would be needed under a flat tax with business income taxed at the source.

The way that we have chosen to set up the business

FIGURE 2–2

Form 2	Business Tax	1996
Business name		Employer Identification Number
Street address		County
City, state, and ZIP code		Principal product

1	Gross revenue from sales	1	
2	Allowable costs		
	(a) Purchases of goods, services, and materials	2a	
	(b) Wages, salaries, and retirement benefits	2b	
	(c) Purchases of capital equipment, structures, and land	2c	
3	Total allowable costs *(sum of lines 2(a), 2(b), and 2(c))*	3	
4	Taxable income *(line 1 less line 3)*	4	
5	Tax *(19% of line 4)*	5	
6	Carry-forward from 1994	6	
7	Interest on carry-forward *(6 % of line 6)*	7	
8	Carry-forward into 1995 *(line 6 plus line 7)*	8	
9	Tax due*(line 5 less line 8, if positive)*	9	
10	Carry-forward to 1996 *(line 8 less line 5, if positive)*	10	

tax is not arbitrary. On the contrary, it is dictated by the principles we set forth at the beginning of this discussion. The tax would be assessed on all the income originating in a business but not on any income that originates in other businesses, nor would it tax the wages, salaries, and pensions paid to employees. The types of income taxed by the business tax would include:

- profits from the use of plant and equipment
- profits from ideas embodied in copyrights, patents,

13

trade secrets, and the like
- profits from past organization-building, marketing, and advertising efforts
- earnings of key executives and others who are owners as well as employees, and who are paid less than they contribute to the business (so that reduced compensation would not be used to avoid taxation)
- earnings of doctors, lawyers, and other professionals who have businesses organized as proprietorships or partnerships
- rent earned from apartments and other real estate
- fringe benefits provided to workers

All a business's income would derive from the sale of its products and services. On the top line of the business tax form (figure 2–2) would appear the gross sales of the business—its proceeds from the sale of all its products. But some of the proceeds would come from the resale of inputs and parts the firm purchased; the tax would already have been paid on these items because the seller also would have to pay the business tax. Thus, the firm could deduct the cost of all the goods, materials, and services it purchased for the purpose of making the product it sells. In addition, it could deduct its wages, salaries, and pensions, for, under our wage tax, the taxes on these would be paid by the workers receiving them. Finally, the business could deduct all its outlays for plant, equipment, and land. Later we will explain why this investment incentive would be just the right one.

Everything left from this calculation is the income originating in the firm and would be taxed at the flat rate of 19 percent. The prospective revenue from the business tax in 1993 would have been the $362 billion we computed earlier. Many deductions allowed to businesses under current laws would be eliminated in our plan, including interest payments and fringe benefits. But our exclusion of these deductions is not an arbitrary move to increase the tax base. In all cases, the elimination of deductions, when combined with the other features of our system, moves toward the goal of taxing all income once at a common, low rate to achieve a broad consumption tax.

Eliminating the deduction for interest paid by businesses is a central part of our general plan to tax business income at the source. It makes sense because we propose not to tax interest received by individuals. The tax that the government now hopes (sometimes in vain) that individuals will pay will assuredly be paid by the business itself.

We sweep away the whole complicated apparatus of depreciation deductions, but we replace it with something more favorable for capital formation, an immediate 100 percent first-year tax write-off of all investment spending. Sometimes this approach is called *expensing* of investment; it is standard in the value-added approach to consumption taxation. In other words, we do not deny depreciation deductions; we enhance them.

Fringe benefits are outside the current tax system entirely, which makes no sense. The cost of these benefits is deductible by businesses, but workers are not taxed on their value. Consequently, fringe benefits have a big advantage over cash wages. As taxation has become heavier and heavier, fringe benefits have become more and more important in the total package offered by employers to workers. Such benefits were only 1.2 percent of total compensation in 1929, when income taxes were unimportant, but reached almost 18 percent in 1993. The explosion of benefits is strictly an artifact of taxation, and benefits are an economically inefficient way to pay workers. If the tax system were neutral, with equal taxes on fringes and cash, workers would rather take their income in cash and make their own decisions about health and life insurance, parking, exercise facilities, and all the other things they now get from their employers without much choice. Further, failing to tax benefits means that taxes on other types of income are higher. Bringing all types of income under the tax system is essential for lower rates.

Under our system, each business would file a simple form. Even the largest business—the General Motors Corporation in 1993, with $138 billion in sales—would fill out our simple postcard form. Every line on the form is a well-defined number obtained directly from the business's accounting records. Line 1, gross revenue from sales, is the actual number of dollars received from the sales of all the products and services sold by the business, plus the proceeds from the sale of plant, equipment, and land. Line 2a is the actual amount paid for all the inputs bought from other businesses necessary for the operation of the business (that is, not passed on to its workers or owners). The firm could report any purchase actually needed for the business's operations and not part of the compensation of workers or owners. Line 2b is the actual cash put in the hands of workers and former workers. All the dollars deducted on this line will have to be reported by the workers on their Form 1 wage-tax returns. Line 2c reports purchases of new and used capital equipment, buildings, and land. Note that the firm would not have to agonize over whether a computer modem is a capital investment or a current input; both are deductible, and the IRS would not care on which line it would appear.

The taxable income computed on line 4 bears little resemblance to anyone's notion of profit. The business tax would not be a profit tax. When a firm is having an outstanding year in sales and profits but is building new factories to handle rapid growth, it might well have a low or even negative taxable income. Later, when expansion slows but sales are at a high level, the income generated at the firm would be taxed at 19 percent.

Because the business tax would treat investment in plant, equipment, and land as an expense, companies in the start-up period would have negative taxable income. But the government would not write a check for the negative tax on the negative income. When the government has a policy of writing checks, clever people abuse the opportunity. Instead, the negative tax would be carried forward to future years, when the business should have positive taxable income. There would be no limit to the number of years of carry forward. Moreover, balances carried forward would earn the market rate of interest (6 percent in 1995). Lines 6 through 10 show the mechanics of the carry-forward process.

Investment Incentives

The high rates of the current tax system significantly impede capital formation. On this point almost all experts agree. The government's solution to the problem has been to add one special investment or saving incentive on top of another, creating a complex and unworkable maze of regulations and tax forms. Existing incentives are appallingly uneven. Capital projects taking full advantage of depreciation deductions and the deductibility of interest paid to organizations exempt from income tax may actually receive subsidies from the government, rather than being taxed. But equity-financed projects are taxed heavily. Investment incentives, together with the deductibility of interest, severely distort the flow of capital into projects eligible for debt finance.

Our idea is to start over, throwing away all the present incentives and replacing them with a simple, uniform principle and treating the total amount of investment as an expense in the year it is made. The entire incentive for capital formation would be on the investment side, instead of the badly fitting split in the current tax system between investment incentives and saving incentives. The first virtue of this reform is simplicity. Businesses and government would not need to quarrel, as they do now, over what is an investment and what is a current expense. The distinction would not matter for the tax. Complicated depreciation calculations, carrying over from one year to the next and driving the small business owner to distraction, would vanish from the tax form. The even more complicated provisions for recapturing depreciation when a piece of equipment or a building is sold would vanish as well, to everyone's relief.

Expensing of investment has a much deeper rationale than simplicity. Every act of investment in the economy ultimately traces back to an act of saving. A tax on income with an exemption for saving is in effect a tax on consumption, for consumption is the difference between income and saving. Consumption is what people take out of the economy; income is what people contribute. A consumption tax is the exact embodiment of the principle that people should be taxed on what they take out, not on what they put in. The flat tax, with expensing of investment, is precisely a consumption tax.

Expensing investment would eliminate the double taxation of saving; this would be another way to express the most economically significant feature of expensing. Under the current income tax, people pay tax once when they earn and save and again when the savings earn a return. With expensing, the first tax would be abolished. For individuals, the return to saving would be, in effect, deducted in computing the tax. Later, this return to saving would be taxed through the business tax. Although economists have dreamed up a number of other ways to eliminate double taxation of saving (involving complicated record keeping and reporting by individuals), the technique exploited in our flat tax is by far the most straightforward.

The easiest case for showing that expensing of investment makes our proposal a consumption tax arises when someone invests directly in a personally owned business. Suppose a taxpayer receives $1,000 in earnings and turns around and buys a piece of business equipment for $1,000. There would be a tax of $190 on the earnings but also a deduction worth $190 in reduced taxes for the equipment purchase. On net, there would be no tax. The taxpayer has not consumed any of the original $1,000 either. Later, the taxpayer would receive business income representing the earnings of the machine. This income would be taxed at 19 percent. If the taxpayer chooses to consume rather than invest again, there would be a 19 percent tax on the consumption. So the total effect would be a 19 percent consumption tax.

Most people do not invest directly by purchasing machines themselves. The U.S. economy has wonderfully developed financial markets for channeling savings from individual savers, on the one hand, to businesses with good investment opportunities, on the other hand. Individuals invest in firms by purchasing shares or bonds, and then the firms purchase plant and equipment. The tax system we propose taxes the consumption of individuals in this environment as well. Suppose the same taxpayer pays the $190 tax on the same $1,000 and puts the remaining $810 into the stock market. For simplicity, suppose that the share pays out to its owner all the aftertax earnings on equipment costing $1,000. That assumption makes sense, because the firm could buy $1,000 worth of equipment with the $810 from our taxpayer plus the tax write-off worth $190 that would come with the equipment purchase. Our taxpayer gets the advantage of the investment write-off even though there is no deduction for the purchase of the share. The market passes through the incentive from the firm to the individual investor.

Another possibility for the taxpayer is to buy a bond for $810. Again, the firm issuing the bond can buy a $1,000 machine with the $810, after taking advantage of the tax deduction. To compete with the returns available in the stock market, however, the bond must pay approximately the same returns as a stock selling for the same price does, which in turn is equal to the aftertax earnings of the machine. It would not matter then how the taxpayer invests the $810. In all cases, there is effectively no tax for saved income; the tax is payable only when the income is consumed.

In our system, any investment, in effect, would have the same economic advantage that a 401(K), IRA, or Keogh account has in the current tax system. And we achieve this desirable goal by *reducing* the amount of record keeping and reporting. Today, taxpayers have to deduct their Keogh and IRA contributions on their Form 1040s, and then they have to report the distributions from the funds as income when they retire. Moreover, proponents of the "cash-flow" consumption tax would extend these requirements to all forms of saving. Our system would accomplish the same goal without any forms or record keeping.

Capital Gains

Capital gains on rental property, plant, and equipment would be taxed under the business tax. The purchase price would be deducted at the time of purchase, and the sale price would be taxed at the time of the sale. Every owner of rental real estate would be required to fill out the simple business tax return, Form 2.

Capital gains would be taxed exclusively at the business level and not at the personal level. In other words, our system would eliminate the double taxation of capital gains inherent in the current tax system. To see how this works, consider the case of the common stock of a corporation. The market value of the stock is the capitalization of its expected future earnings. Because the owners of the stock will receive their earnings after the corporation has paid the business tax, the market capitalizes expected aftertax earnings. A capital gain occurs when the market perceives that prospective aftertax earnings have risen. When the higher earnings materialize in the future, they will be correspondingly taxed. A tax system like the current one, with both an income tax and a capital gains tax, imposes double taxation. The goal of taxing all income exactly once can best be achieved by placing an airtight tax on the income at the source. With taxation at the source, it is inappropriate and inefficient to tax capital gains as they occur at the destination.

Another way to see that capital gains should not be taxed separately under the flat tax is to look at the national income accounts. Gross domestic product, the most comprehensive measure of the nation's command over resources, does not include capital gains. The base of the flat tax is GDP minus investment, that is, consumption. To include capital gains in the flat-tax base would depart from the principle that it is a tax on consumption.

Capital gains on owner-occupied houses are not taxed under our proposal. Very few capital gains on houses are actually taxed under the current system. Gains can be rolled over, there is an exclusion for older home sellers, and gains are never taxed at death. Exclusion of capital gains on houses makes sense because state and local governments put substantial property taxes on houses in relation to their values. Adding a capital gains tax on top of property taxes is double taxation in the same way that adding a capital gains tax on top of an income tax is double taxation of business income.

Imports, Exports, and Multinational Business

With the North American Free Trade Agreement and the growth of trade throughout the world, U.S. companies are doing more and more business in other countries, and foreign companies are increasingly active here. Should the U.S. government try to tax business operations in other countries owned by Americans? And should it tax foreign-owned operations in the United States? These are increasingly controversial questions. Under the current tax system, foreign operations of U.S. companies are taxed in principle, but the taxpayer receives a credit against U.S. taxes for taxes paid to the country where the business operates. Because the current tax system is based on a confused combination of taxing some income at the origin and some at the destination, taxation of foreign operations is messy.

Under the consistent application of taxing all business income at the source, the flat tax embodies a clean solution to the problems of multinational operations. The flat tax would apply only to the domestic operations of all businesses, whether of domestic, foreign, or mixed ownership. Only the revenue from the sales of products within the United States plus the value of products as they are exported would be reported on line 1 of Form 2. Only the costs of labor, materials, and other inputs purchased in the United States or imported to the United States would be allowable on line 2 as deductions for the business tax. Physical presence in the United States is the simple rule that determines whether a purchase or sale is included in taxable revenue or allowable cost.

To see how the business tax would apply to foreign trade, consider first an importer selling its wares within the United States. Its costs would include the actual amount it paid for its imports, valued as they entered the country. This would generally be the actual amount paid for them in the country of their origin. Its revenue would be the actual receipts from sales in the United States. Second, consider an exporter selling goods produced here to foreigners. Its costs would be all the inputs and compensation paid in the United States, and its revenue would be the amount received from sales to foreigners, provided that the firm did not add to the product after it departed the country. Third, consider a firm that sends parts to Mexico for assembly and brings back the final product for sale in the United States. The value of the parts as they leave here would count as part of the revenue of the firm, and the value of the assembled product as it returned would be an expense. The firm, for example, would not deduct the actual costs of its Mexican assembly plant.

Under the principle of taxing only domestic activities, the U.S. tax system would mesh neatly with the tax systems of our major trading partners. If every nation used the flat tax, all income throughout the world would be taxed once and only once. Because the basic principle of the flat tax is already in use in the many nations with value-added taxes, a U.S. flat tax would harmonize with those foreign tax systems.

Application of the wage tax, Form 1, in the world economy would follow the same principle. All earnings from work in the United States would be taxed, irrespective of the worker's citizenship, but the tax would not apply to the foreign earnings of Americans.

Choices about the international location of businesses and employment are influenced by differences in tax rates. The United States, with a low tax rate of 19 percent, would be much the most attractive location among major industrial nations from the point of view of taxation. Although the flat tax would not tax the overseas earnings of American workers and businesses, there is no reason to fear an exodus of economic activity. On the contrary, the favorable tax climate in the United States would draw in new business from everywhere in the world.

The Transition

In our flat tax proposal, we are spending the bulk of our effort in laying out a good, practical tax system. We have not made concessions to the political pressures that may well force the nation to accept an improved tax system that falls short of the ideal we have in mind. One area where the political process is likely to complicate our simple proposal is the transition from the current tax to the flat tax. The transition issues that are likely to draw the most attention are depreciation and interest deductions. In both cases, taxpayers who made plans and commitments before the tax reform will cry loudly for special provisions to continue the deductions.

Congress will face a choice between denying taxpayers the deductions they expected before tax reform or granting the deductions and raising the tax rate to make up for the lost revenue. Fortunately, this is a temporary problem. Once existing capital is fully depreciated and existing borrowing paid off, any special transition provisions can be taken off the books.

Depreciation Deductions. Existing law lets businesses deduct the cost of an investment on a declining schedule over many years. From the point of view of the business, multiyear depreciation deductions are not as attractive as the first-year write-off prescribed in the flat tax. No business will complain about the flat tax as far as future investment is concerned. But businesses may well protest the unexpected elimination of the unused depreciation they thought they would be able to take on the plant and equipment they installed before the tax reform. Without special transition provisions, these deductions would simply be lost.

How much is at stake? In 1992, total depreciation deductions under the personal and corporate income taxes came to $597 billion. At the 34 percent rate for most corporations (which is close to the rate paid by the individuals who are likely to take deductions as proprietors or partners), those deductions were worth $192 billion. At the 19 percent flat rate, the deductions would be worth only $108 billion.

If Congress chose to honor all unused depreciation from investment predating tax reform, it would take about $597 billion out of the tax base for 1995. To raise the same amount of revenue as our original 19 percent rate would, the tax rate would have to rise to about 20.1 percent.

Honoring past depreciation would mollify business interest, especially in industries with large amounts of unused depreciation for past investment but little prospect of large first-year write-offs for future investment. In addition, it would buttress the government's credibility in tax matters by carrying through on a past promise to give a tax incentive for investment. On the other hand, the move would require a higher tax rate and a less efficient economy in the future.

If Congress did opt to honor past depreciation, it should recognize that the higher tax rate needed to make up for the lost revenue is temporary. Within five years, the bulk of the existing capital would be depreciated, and the tax rate should be brought back to 19 percent. From the outset, the tax rate should be committed to drop to 19 percent as soon as the transition depreciation is paid off.

Interest Deductions. Loss of interest deductions and elimination of interest taxation are two of the most conspicuous features of our tax reform plan. During the transition, there will be winners and losers from the change, and Congress is sure to hear from the losers. Congress may well decide to adopt a temporary transitional measure to help them. Such a measure need not compromise the principles of the flat tax or lessen its contribution to improved efficiency.

Our tax reform proposal calls for the parallel removal of interest deductions and interest taxation. If a transitional measure allows the continuation of deductions for interest on outstanding debt, it should also require the continuation of taxation of that interest as income of the lender. If all deductions are completely matched with taxation on the other side, then a transition provision to protect existing interest deductions would have *no* effect on revenue. In that respect, interest deductions are easier to handle in the transition than are depreciation deductions.

If Congress decides that a transitional measure to protect interest deductions is needed, we suggest the following. Any borrower may choose to treat interest payments as a tax deduction. If the borrower so chooses, the lender *must* treat the interest as taxable income. But the borrower's deduction should be only 90 percent of the actual interest payment, while the lender's taxable income should include 100 percent of the interest receipts.

Under this transitional plan, borrowers would be protected for almost all their existing deductions. Someone whose personal finances would become untenable if the mortgage-interest deduction were suddenly eliminated can surely get through with 90 percent of the earlier deduction. But the plan builds in an incentive for renegotiating the interest payments along the lines we discussed earlier. Suppose a family is paying $10,000 in annual mortgage interest. They could stick with this payment and deduct $9,000 of it per year. Their net cost, after subtracting the value of their deduction with the 19 percent tax rate, would be $8,290. The net income to the bank, after subtracting the 19 percent tax it pays on the whole $10,000, would be $8,100. Alternatively, the family could accept an arrangement proposed by the bank: the interest payment would be lowered to $8,200 by rewriting the mortgage. The family would agree to forgo the right to deduct the interest, and the bank would no longer have to pay tax on the interest. Now the couple's cost will be $8,200 (instead of $8,290 without the arrangement) and the bank's income will be $8,200 (instead of $8,100). The family will come out $90 ahead, and the bank will come out $100 ahead. The arrangement would be beneficial to both.

One of the attractive features of this plan is that it does not have to make any distinctions between old borrowing, existing at the time of the tax reform, and new borrowing, arranged after the reform. Lenders would always require that new borrowers opt out of their deductions and would thus offer a correspondingly lower interest rate. Otherwise, the lender would be saddled with a tax bill larger than the tax deduction received by the borrower.

As far as revenue is concerned, this plan would actually add a bit to federal revenue in comparison with the pure flat tax. Whenever a borrower exercised the right to deduct interest, the government would collect more revenue from the lender than it would lose from the borrower. As more and more arrangements were rewritten to eliminate deductions and to lower interest, the excess revenue would disappear, and we would be left with the pure flat tax.

Variants of the Flat Tax

In this proposal, we have set forth what we think is the best flat tax. But our ideas are more general than this specific proposal. The same principles could be applied with different choices about the key trade-offs. The two most important trade-offs are:

- *Progressivity versus tax rate.* A higher personal allowance would put an even lower burden on low- and middle-income families. But it would require a higher tax rate.

• *Investment incentives versus tax rate.* If the business tax had less than full write-off for purchases of capital goods, the tax rate could be lower.

Here are some alternative combinations of allowances and tax rates that would all raise the same amount of revenue:

Allowance for Family of Four	Tax Rate
$12,500	15%
$22,500	19%
$34,500	23%

The choice among these alternatives depends on beliefs about how the burden of taxes should be distributed and on the degree of inefficiency that will be brought into the economy by the corresponding tax rates.

Here are some alternative combinations of investment write-offs and tax rates that would all raise the same amount of revenue:

Equipment Write-off	Structures Write-off	Tax Rate
100%	100%	19%
75%	50%	18%
50%	25%	17%

The choice among these alternatives depends on the sensitivity of investment and saving to incentives and on the degree of inefficiency brought by the tax rate.

Stimulus to Growth

The flat tax at a low, uniform rate of 19 percent will improve the performance of the U.S. economy. Improved incentives to work through increased take-home wages will stimulate work effort and raise total output. Rational investment incentives will raise the total level of investment and channel it into the most productive areas. And sharply lower taxation of entrepreneurial effort will enhance this critical input to the economy.

Work Effort. About two-thirds of today's taxpayers enjoy the low-income tax rate of 15 percent enacted in 1986. Under the flat tax, more than half these taxpayers would face zero tax rates because their total family earnings would fall short of the exemption amount ($22,500 for a family of four). The other half would face a slight increase in their tax rates on the margin, from 15 percent to 19 percent. In 1991, the remaining third of taxpayers were taxed at rates of 28 and 31 percent, and the addition of the 39.6 percent bracket in 1992 worsened incentives further. Heavily taxed people earn a disproportionate share of income: in 1991, 58 percent of all earnings were taxed at rates of 28 percent or higher. The net effect of the flat tax, with marginal rates of 0 and 19 percent, would be to improve incentives dramatically for almost everyone who is economically active.

One point we need to emphasize is that a family's marginal tax rate determines its incentives for all types of economic activity. There is much confusion on this point. Some authors, for example, have written that a married woman faces a special disincentive because the marginal tax on the first dollar of her earnings is the same as the marginal tax on the last dollar of her husband's earnings. It is true that incentives to work for a woman with a well-paid husband are seriously eroded by high tax rates. But so are her husband's incentives. What matters for both of their decisions is how much of any extra dollar of earnings they will keep after taxes. Under the U.S. income tax, with joint filing, the fraction either of them takes home after taxes is always the same, no matter how their earnings are split between them.

Sheer hours of work make up one of the most important dimensions of productive effort and one that is known to be sensitive to incentives. At first, it may seem difficult for people to alter the amount of work they supply to the economy. Aren't most jobs forty hours a week, fifty-two weeks a year? It turns out that only a fraction of the work force is restricted in that way. Most of us face genuine decisions about how much to work. Teenagers and young adults—in effect anyone before the responsibilities of parenthood—typically work much less than full time for the full year. Improving their incentives could easily make them switch from part-time to full-time work or cause them to spend less time taking it easy between jobs.

Married women remain one of the largest underused resources in the U.S. economy, although a growing fraction enters the labor market each year. In 1993, only 58 percent of all women over fifteen were at work or looking for work; the remaining 42 percent were spending their time at home or in school but could be drawn into the market if the incentives were right. There is no doubt about the sensitivity of married women to economic incentives. Studies show a systematic tendency for women with low aftertax wages and high-income husbands to work little. Those with high aftertax wages and lower-income husbands work a lot. It is thus reasonable to infer that sharply reduced marginal tax rates on married women's earnings will further stimulate their interest in the market.

Another remarkable source of unused labor power in the United States is men who have taken early retirement. Although 92 percent of men aged twenty-five to fifty-four are in the labor force, only 65 percent of those from fifty-five to sixty-four are at work or looking for work and just 17 percent of those over sixty-five. Again, retirement is very much a matter of incentives. High marginal taxation of earnings discourages many perfectly fit men from continuing to work. Because mature men are among the best paid in the economy, a great many of them face marginal tax rates of 28, 36, or even 40 percent. Reduction to a uniform

19 percent could significantly reduce early retirement and make better use of the skills of older men.

Economists have devoted a great deal of effort to measuring the potential stimulus to work from tax reform. The consensus is that all groups of workers would respond to the flat tax by raising their work effort. A few workers would reduce their hours either because the flat rate would exceed their current marginal rate or because reform would add so much to their incomes that they would feel that earning was less urgent. But the great majority would face much improved incentives. The smallest expected responses are from adult men and the largest from married women.

In light of the research on labor supply, were we to switch from the current tax law to our proposed flat tax, a reasonable projection is an increase of about 4 percent in total hours of work in the U.S. economy. That increase would mean about 1.5 hours per week on the average but would take the form of second jobs for some workers, more weeks of work per year for others, and more hours per week for those working part time. The total annual output of goods and services in the U.S. economy would rise by about 3 percent, or almost $200 billion. That is nearly $750 per person, an astonishing sum. Of course, it might take some time for the full influence of improved incentives to have their effect. But the bottom line is unambiguous: tax reform would have an important favorable effect on total work effort.

Capital Formation. Economists are far from agreement on the impact of tax reform on investment. As we have stressed earlier, the existing system puts heavy tax rates on business income, even though the net revenue from the system is small. These rates seriously erode investment incentives. Generous but erratic investment provisions in the current law and lax enforcement of taxes on business income at the personal level, however, combine to limit the adverse impact. The current tax system subsidizes investment through tax-favored entities such as pension funds, while it taxes capital formation heavily if it takes the form of new businesses. The result has been to sustain capital formation at reasonably high levels but to channel the investment into inefficient uses.

The most important structural bias of the existing system is the double taxation of business income earned in corporations and paid out to shareholders. Double taxation dramatically reduces the incentive to create new businesses in risky lines where debt financing is not available. On the other side, the existing system places no current tax on investments that can be financed by debt, where the debt is held by pension funds or other nontaxed entities. The result is a huge twist in incentives, away from entrepreneurial activities and toward safe, debt-financed activities.

The flat tax would eliminate the harmful twist in the current tax system. The flat tax has a single, uniform incentive for investment of all types; businesses would treat all purchases of capital equipment and buildings as expenses. As we noted earlier, allowing immediate write-off of investment is the ideal investment incentive. Taxing all income evenly and allowing expensing of investment amount to a tax on consumption. Public finance economists Alan Auerbach and Laurence Kotlikoff estimate that the use of a flat-rate consumption tax in place of an income tax would raise the ratio of capital stock to GDP from 5.0 to 6.2. Other economists are less optimistic that the correction of the double taxation of saving would provide the resources for this large an increase in investment. But all agree that there would be *some* favorable effect on capital formation.

In terms of added GDP, the increase in the capital stock projected by Auerbach and Kotlikoff would translate into 6 percent more goods and services. Not all this extra growth would occur within the seven-year span we are looking at. But, even allowing for only partial attainment in seven years and for a possible overstatement in their work, it seems reasonable to predict a 2 to 4 percent increase in GDP on account of added capital formation within seven years.

Tax reform would improve the productivity of capital by directing investment to the most productive uses. Auerbach has demonstrated, in a paper published by the Brookings Institution, that the bias of the current tax system toward equipment and away from structures imposes a small but important burden on the economy. The flat tax would correct this bias. Auerbach estimates that the correction would be equivalent to a 3.2 percent increase in the capital stock. GDP would rise on this account by 0.8 percent.

Entrepreneurial Incentives and Effort. U.S. economic growth has slowed in the past two decades, and surely one reason is the confiscatory taxation of successful endeavors and the tax subsidy for safe, nonentrepreneurial undertakings. There are not any scholarly studies with quantitative conclusions on the general benefits from a fundamental shift, but they could be large.

Today's tax system punishes entrepreneurs. Part of the trouble comes from the interest deduction. The people in the driver's seat in the capital market, where money is loaned and borrowed, are those who lend out money on behalf of institutions and those who have figured out how to avoid paying income tax on their interest. These people do not like insecure loans to new businesses based on great new ideas. They do like lending secured to readily marketable assets by mortgages or similar arrangements. It is easy to borrow from a pension fund to build an apartment building, buy a boxcar, put up a shopping center, or anything else where the fund can foreclose and sell the asset in case the borrower defaults. Funds will not lend money to entrepreneurs with new ideas because the lenders are unable to evaluate what they could sell off in case of a default.

Entrepreneurs can and do raise money the hard way, by giving equity interests to investors. An active venture capital market operates for exactly this purpose. But the cost to the entrepreneur is high: the ownership given to the financial backers deprives the entrepreneur of the full gain in case things work out well.

Even with the best tax system, or no taxes at all, entrepreneurs of course would not be able to borrow with ordinary bonds or loans and thus capture the entire future profits of a new business. It is not easy to get other people to put money into a risky, innovative business. Equity participation by investors is a fact of life. But the perverse tax system greatly worsens the incentives for entrepreneurs. The combination of corporate and personal taxation of equity investments is actually close to confiscation. The owners of a successful new business are taxed first when the profits flow in, at 34 percent, and again when the returns make their way to the entrepreneur and the other owners. All of them are likely to be in the 40 percent bracket for the personal income tax, making the combined effective tax rate close to 60 percent. The entrepreneur first gives a large piece of the action to the inactive owners who put up the capital and then surrenders well over half the remainder to the government.

The prospective entrepreneur will likely be attracted to the easier life of the investor who uses borrowed money. How much easier it is to put up a shopping center, borrow from a pension fund or insurance company, and deduct everything paid to the inactive investor!

Today's discriminatory system taxes entrepreneurial success at 60 percent while it actually subsidizes leveraged investment. Our simple tax would put the same low rate on both activities. A huge redirection of national effort would follow. And the redirection could only be good for national income. While shopping centers, apartment buildings, airplanes, boxcars, medical equipment, and cattle have their place, tax advantages have made us invest far too much in them, and their contribution to income is correspondingly low. Real growth will come when effort and capital flow back into innovation and the development of new businesses, the areas where taxation has discouraged investment. The contribution to income from new resources will be correspondingly high.

Total Potential Growth from Improved Incentives. We project a 3 percent increase in output from increased total work in the U.S. economy and an additional increment to total output of 3 percent from added capital formation and dramatically improved entrepreneurial incentives. The sum of 6 percent is our best estimate of the improvement in real incomes after the economy has had seven years to assimilate the changed economic conditions brought about by the simple flat tax. Both the amount and the timing are conservative.

Even this limited claim for economic improvement represents enormous progress. By 2002, it would mean that the income of each American would be about $1,900 higher, in 1995 dollars, as a consequence of tax reform.

Interest Rates

The flat tax would pull down interest rates immediately. Today's high rates are sustained partly by the income-tax deduction for interest paid and the tax on interest earned. The tax benefit ameliorates much of the pain of high interest, and the IRS takes part of the income from interest. Borrowers tolerate high interest rates and lenders require them. The simple tax would permit no deduction for interest paid and put no tax on interest received. Interest payments throughout the economy would be flows of aftertax income, thanks to taxation of business income at the source.

With the flat tax, borrowers would no longer be so tolerant of interest payments, and lenders would no longer be concerned about taxes. The meeting of minds in the credit market, where borrowing equals lending, would inevitably occur at a lower interest rate. Potentially, the fall could be spectacular. Much borrowing is done by corporations and wealthy individuals, who face marginal tax rates of 34 and 40 percent. The wealthy, however, almost by definition, are the big lenders in the economy. If every lender and every borrower were in the 40 percent bracket, a tax reform eliminating deduction and taxation of interest would cut interest rates by a factor of 0.4—for example, from 10 to 6 percent. But the leakage problem in the United States is so great that the actual drop in interest would be far short of this huge potential. So much lending comes through the devices by which the well-to-do get their interest income under low tax rates that a drop by a factor of 0.4 would be impossible. Lenders taxed at low rates would be worse off if taxation were eliminated but interest rates fell by half. In an economy with lenders enjoying low marginal rates before reform, the meeting of the minds would have to come at an interest rate well above 0.6 times the prereform level. But the decline would be at least a fifth—say, from 10 percent to 8 percent. Reform would bring a noticeable drop in interest rates.

One direct piece of evidence is municipal bonds, which yield interest not taxed under the federal income tax. Tax reform would make all bonds like tax-free municipals, so the current rates on municipals give a hint about the level of all interest rates after reform. In 1994, municipals yielded about one-sixth less interest than comparable taxable bonds. But this is a conservative measure of the likely fall in interest rates after reform. Today, tax-free rates are kept high because there are so many opportunities to own taxable bonds in low-tax ways. Why own a bond from the city of Los Angeles paying 6 percent tax free when an investor can create a personal pension fund and hold a Pacific Telesis bond paying 7 percent? Interest rates could easily fall to three-quarters of their present levels after tax reform; rates on tax-free securities would then fall a little as well.

The decline in interest rates brought about by putting interest on an aftertax basis would not by itself change the economy very much. To Ford Motors, contemplating borrowing to finance a modern plant, the attraction of lower rates would be offset by the cost of lost interest deductions. But the flat tax would do much more than put interest on an aftertax basis. Tax rates on corporations would be slashed to a uniform 19 percent from the double taxation of a 34 percent corporate rate on top of a personal rate of up to 40 percent. And investment incentives will be improved through the first-year write-off. All told, borrowing for investment purposes would become a better deal. As the likely investment boom develops, borrowing will rise and will tend to push up interest rates. In principle, interest rates could rise to their prereform levels but only if the boom is vigorous. We cannot be sure what would happen to interest rates after tax reform, but we can be sure that high-interest, low-investment stagnation would not occur. Either interest rates will fall or investment will take off.

As a safe working hypothesis, we will assume that interest rates fall in the year after tax reform by about a fifth, say, from 10 to 8 percent. We assume a quiescent underlying economy, not perturbed by sudden shifts in monetary policy, government spending, or oil prices. Now, take a look at borrowing decisions made before and after reform. Suppose a prereform entrepreneur is considering an investment yielding $1 million a year in revenue and involving $800,000 in interest costs at 10 percent interest. Today the entrepreneur pays a 40 percent tax on the net income of $200,000, giving an aftertax cash flow of $120,000. After reform, the entrepreneur would earn the same $1 million and pay $640,000 interest on the same principal at 8 percent. There would be a 19 percent tax on the earnings without deducting interest; the amount of the tax is $190,000. Aftertax income is $1,000,000 − $640,000 − $190,000 = $170,000, well above the $120,000 before reform. Reform is to the entrepreneur's advantage and to the advantage of capital formation. Gains from the lower tax rate more than make up for losses from denial of the interest deduction.

How can it be that both the entrepreneur and the government come out ahead from the tax reform? They do not: one element is missing from this accounting. Before the reform, the government collected some tax on the interest paid by the entrepreneur—potentially as much as 40 percent of the $800,000. But, as our stories about leakage make clear, the government is actually lucky to get a small fraction of that potential.

To summarize, the flat tax would automatically lower interest rates. Without an interest deduction, borrowers require lower costs. Without an interest tax, lenders are satisfied with lower payments. The simple flat tax would have an important effect on interest rates. Lower interest rates would also stimulate the housing market, offsetting the absence of the mortgage interest deduction, as will be explained below.

Housing. Everyone who hears about the flat tax, with no deductions for interest, worries about its effect on the housing market. Won't the elimination of the deduction depress the prices of existing houses and impoverish the homeowner who can afford a house only because of its interest deductions? Our answer to all these questions is no, but we freely concede that that issue is significant.

In all but the long run, house prices are set by the demand for houses, because the supply can change only slowly. If tax reform increases the cost of carrying a house of given value, then demand will fall, and house prices will fall correspondingly. For this reason, we will look closely at what happens to carrying costs before and after tax reform.

If tax reform had no effect on interest rates, its adverse effect on carrying costs and house values would be a foregone conclusion. A $200,000 house with a $120,000 mortgage at 10 percent has interest costs of $12,000 per year before deductions and $8,640 after deductions (for someone in the 28 percent tax bracket). The monthly carrying cost is $720. Take away the deductions, and the carrying cost jumps to $12,000 per year or $1,000 per month. Inevitably, the prospective purchaser faced with this change would have to settle for a cheaper house. Collectively, the reluctance of purchasers would bring house prices down so that the buyers could afford the houses on the market.

As we stressed earlier, our tax reform will immediately lower interest rates. And lower rates bring higher house prices, a point dramatically impressed on homeowners in the early 1980s when big increases in interest severely dampened the housing market. The total effect of reform will depend on the relative strengths of the contending forces—the value of the lost interest deduction against the value of lower interest. We have good reasons to think that interest rates would fall by about two percentage points—say, from 10 to 8 percent for mortgages. The value of the lost deduction, in contrast, depends on just what fraction of a house a prospective purchaser intends to finance. First-time home buyers typically, but not always, finance three-quarters or more of the price of a house. Some of them have family money or other wealth and make larger down payments. Families moving up by selling existing houses generally plan much larger equity positions in their new houses. Perhaps a down payment of 50 percent is the average, so families are paying interest (and deducting) on $500 per thousand dollars of house.

A second determinant of the carrying cost is the value of the deduction, set by the marginal tax rate. Among homeowners, a marginal rate of 28 percent is typical, corresponding to a taxable income of $37,000 to $89,000. Interest-carrying costs per thousand dollars of house are $50 per year before taxes ($500 borrowed at 10 percent interest) and $36 per year after taxes. When tax reform comes, the interest rate will fall to 8 percent, and carrying costs will be $40 per thousand per year ($500 at 8 percent) both

before and after taxes. Tax reform will put this buyer behind by $4 per thousand dollars of house per year, or $800
per year for the $100,000 house.

If this $800 per year were the end of the story, it would
bring a modest decline in house prices. But there is another factor we have not touched on yet. The buyer's equity position—the down payment—must come from
somewhere. By putting wealth into a house, the buyer sac-
rifices the return that wealth would have earned elsewhere.
The alternative return from the equity in the house is another component of the carrying cost. Tax reform would
almost surely reduce that component. As just one example,
take a prospective buyer who could put wealth into an
untaxed retirement fund if he did not put it into a house.
The fund holds bonds; after reform, the interest rate on
bonds would be perhaps three percentage points lower,
and so the implicit cost of the equity would be lower by the
same amount.

To take a conservative estimate, tax reform might
lower the implicit cost of equity by one percentage point
as interest rates fall. Then the carrying costs of the buyer's
equity would decline by $5 ($500 at 1 percent) per thousand dollars of house per year. Recall that the buyer has
come out behind by $4 on the mortgage-interest side. On
net, tax reform would *lower* the carrying costs by $5 - $4 =
$1 per thousand, or $200 per year for the $200,000 house.
Then housing prices would actually rise under the impe-
tus of tax reform.

We will not argue that tax reform per se would stimulate the housing market. But we do believe that the potential effects on house prices would be small, small enough
to be lost in the ups and downs of a volatile market. Basically, reform would have two effects: to reduce interest rates
and related costs of funds (and so to stimulate housing
and other asset markets) and to deny interest deductions
(and so to depress housing). To a reasonable approxima-
tion, these influences will cancel each other out.

If tax reform sets off a rip-roaring investment boom,

interest rates might rise in the years following the immediate drop at the time of the reform. During this period, when corporations will be competing strongly with home buyers for available funds, house prices would lag behind an otherwise brisk economy. The same thing happened in the great investment boom of the late 1960s. But to get the strong economy and new jobs that go with an investment boom, minor disappointments in housing values would seem a reasonable price. In the long run, higher incomes will bring a stronger housing market.

What about the construction industry? Will a slump in new housing accompany a tax reform that banishes interest deductions, as the industry fears? The fate of the industry depends intimately on the price of existing housing. Were tax reform to depress housing by raising carrying costs, the public's interest in new houses would fall in parallel with its diminished enthusiasm for existing houses. Because tax reform will *not* dramatically alter carrying costs in one direction or another, it will not enrich or impoverish the construction industry.

So far, we have looked at the way prospective buyers might calculate what value of house they can afford. These calculations are the proximate determinants of house prices. But they have no bearing on the situation of an existing homeowner who has no intention of selling or buying. To the homeowner, loss of the tax deduction would be pure grief.

Our transition proposal takes care of the problem of existing mortgages without compromising the principles of the flat tax or diminishing its revenue. Homeowners would have the right to continue deducting 90 percent of their mortgage interest. Recall that the bank would then be required to pay tax on the interest it received, even though interest on new mortgages would be untaxed. Homeowners could expect to receive attractive propositions from their banks to rewrite their mortgages at an interest rate about three percentage points lower, but without tax deductibility. Even if banks and homeowners could not get together to lower rates, homeowners could still deduct 90 percent of what they deducted before.

Conclusions

The flat tax comes with strong recommendations. It would bring a drastic simplification of the tax system. It imposes an across-the-board consumption tax at the low rate of 19 percent. It raises enough revenue to replace the existing personal and corporate income taxes. Through consistent use of the source principle of taxation, it would drastically limit the leakage that pervades today's taxes based on the destination principle. The flat tax is progressive: it exempts the poor from paying any tax and imposes a tax that is a rising share of income for other taxpayers. The economy would thrive under the improved incentives that the flat tax would provide.

Note

1.*Editor's Note:* To economists, a consumption tax is frequently described as a tax on wages plus a tax on capital. A flat tax is a consumption tax because it taxes wages to individuals and it taxes capital income minus investment to firms. For a simple explanation as to why the flat tax is a consumption tax, see Jane Gravelle, "The Flat Tax and Other Proposals: Who Will Bear the Tax Burden," in *Tax Notes,* December 18, 1995.

3

The Proposed Sales and Wages Tax—Fair, Flat, or Foolish?

Robert Eisner

The Hall-Rabushka-Armey proposed "flat tax" is not entirely fair. It is not entirely flat. And it is not entirely foolish.

The proposal is touted as bringing almost incredible simplicity to our incredibly complicated federal income tax system. It is also claimed that it will bring significant, major gains to the efficiency and productivity of our economy. And it is argued that by reasonable standards it is fair—fairer than what we have.

That it would bring enormous simplification I will not challenge. And that our current system is a mess I would not dream of denying. I am happy to stipulate that we waste many billions of person-hours and hundreds of billions of dollars in administering, complying with, and

I am indebted to Tom Petska and the staff of the Statistics of Income Division of the Internal Revenue Service for making available and offering some guidance to a number of Statistics of Income documents bearing on the components of income and their taxation. I am also indebted to Eric Toder and the professional staff of the Office of Tax Analysis of the Treasury Department for advice on a number of published documents and general information bearing on the issues discussed in this chapter, and to Robert S. Chirinko for comments on a penultimate draft. And finally, I am grateful for the research assistance of Jim Gill and Jay Hoffman, who have helped process a variety of statistical tabulations, and to Suken Shah for assistance in editing the final tabular presentations.

seeking to avoid or evade current income taxes. Eliminating the current system would indeed add measurably to unemployment as it destroyed the livelihood of hundreds of thousands of tax preparers and accountants, lawyers, and lobbyists.

I am further willing to stipulate that elimination of our current income tax system would rid the economy of countless distortions that lead to misallocation of resources—as between work and leisure and between saving and consumption and among forms of saving and consumption and investment goods.

And I am also willing to stipulate that there is a great deal that reasonable people must find palpably unfair about our present system. It fails over and over again with regard to our usual criteria of horizontal and vertical equity. People with the same incomes pay vastly different amounts of taxes. Many people with very high incomes pay little or nothing in taxes. The progressivity of our tax system as a whole is far less than is generally presumed. If we include all income, we find that the very rich pay smaller proportions of their income in taxes than the moderately rich.

I join too in deploring some of the high marginal tax rates in our current system, although I see the problem somewhat differently from those who seem to note and be concerned with only the marginal income taxes on the top 1 or 2 percent of the income distribution, rates that now reach 39.6 percent and more. I shall come back to this matter but might just point out now that the problem is worse for wage income than for other income and is much worse at the very low end of the income distribution. The marginal effective rate of taxation and loss of benefits for work by many of the very poor on welfare, at least without the earned income tax credit, has been over 100 percent.

With all my stipulations and agreement over the deficiencies of our present income tax system and many of the advantages of the flat tax, I might be tempted to give up and end the debate right here. If I had to choose one or the other, the proposed flat tax or what we have now, I would be sorely tried.

The Proposal

Unfortunately, in its current form, the proposed flat tax has too many objectionable features to allow me to endorse it. These relate considerably to fairness—both horizontal and vertical equity. But they also involve issues of efficiency: as proposed, the flat tax substitutes serious new distortions for those it would eliminate. And without offering substitutes, it eliminates much public intervention, which I, and probably many others, might hesitate to discard cavalierly.

I shall focus my discussion on the Armey tax proposal in H.R. 4585. Where it is not sufficiently spelled out, I shall assume that it is intended to embody the provisions of the Hall-Rabushka proposal.[1] In brief, the proposal would replace current individual and corporate income taxes and all their rates, exclusions, and deductions with two new taxes, one on wage income and one on business.

The Armey proposal would set the "flat" rate on both initially at 20 percent (but drop it to 17 percent in 1997 on the basis of other spending reductions and the expected increase in productivity and resultant tax revenue increases). Hall and Rabushka would set the rate at 19 percent. The wage tax would apply to all wages, salaries, and pensions. The Armey bill would allow deductions on the wage tax totaling $34,700 for a family of four; the Hall and Rabushka "personal allowances" would come to $25,500 for a family of four. There would be no further deductions, none: not for state and local taxes, individual retirement accounts, charitable contributions, mortgage interest, excess health costs, moving expenses—they would all be gone.

The business tax would apply to gross revenue from sales minus allowable costs, which would include purchases of goods, services, and materials; wages, salaries, and retirement benefits; and purchases of capital equipment, structures, and land. Note that capital acquisitions would be "expensed"; there would be no depreciation or separate capital account. Sales of capital equipment, structures, and land, however, would be included in gross revenue. Income from investment would not be included, but banks and insurance companies would, in Hall and Rabushka, have their sales grossed up to include the value of services furnished in lieu of interest payments. Fringe benefits, other than the payment of pensions, would not be deductible, nor would employer contributions for social security and state and local taxes. Neither interest payments nor dividend payouts would be deductible, but neither would be taxable, at the individual level, where only wages and pensions (and not social security benefits) would be taxed.

The Armey bill eliminates withholding taxes, which would appear to invite considerable evasion by wage earners and consequent revenue loss. Hall and Rabushka do provide for withholding and would explicitly eliminate inheritance taxes. Both would eliminate all capital gains taxes (other than that portion of net business taxes that might result from sale of assets for amounts greater than the deductions entailed by their original purchase). Noncorporate business would be subject to the same business tax as corporations; wages and salaries that owners pay to themselves would be deductible on the business tax but taxable (beyond the standard deductions or personal allowances) on the wage tax. Both Armey and Hall and Rabushka have set rates and deductions that they believe would generate revenues equal to those under the current system. Hall and Rabushka use a figure for wages, salaries, and pensions of $3,100 billion, calculate their "family allowances" at $1,705 billion, and thus have a wage tax base of $1,395 billion. They calculate their business tax base at $1,903 billion. Applying a 19 percent rate, they report a flat tax revenue of $627 billion (actually $626.62 billion), which is approximately the total of personal and corporate income taxes in 1993. The Armey proposal claim

45

of revenue neutrality, however, is not consistent with the Hall and Rabushka calculations.[2]

The first point I should make is that what has been proposed is the substitution of a consumption tax for a large part of the current income tax. That is a major part of its import. We could have a flat tax on all income. We could have a consumption tax with progressive rates.[3] Hall and Rabushka and Armey (H-R-A) offer us a "flat" consumption tax, albeit one on domestic consumption only. We may oppose H-R-A not because we reject flat taxes but because we want a flat income tax. We may oppose them not because we oppose a consumption tax but because we prefer a progressive one on income minus saving, which would not have the effect of raising the general level of prices with the various implications for incidence that such a rise would entail.

The second point to be made is that we can eliminate the myriad exemptions, deductions, credits, and other complications in the income tax without going to a consumption tax. And we can eliminate virtually all the complications as well without having a flat tax. The proposed tax actually has two rates, of course, zero up to the amount of deductions, $34,700 for a family of four and 20 percent above that amount, in the Armey bill. We could readily add another rate on upper incomes or wages, say, 28 percent as in the law until 1990, on wages over $69,400, and increase the deductions or lower the 20 percent rate. We could accomplish most of our other objectives but have a somewhat more progressive incidence.

Viewed as a Consumption Tax

Hall and Rabushka explain that their flat tax is in reality a consumption tax because income comes from production but taxes are imposed on total income minus investment. Since saving equals investment, their tax is a consumption tax. In fact, this is not entirely right. Private saving is not equal to gross private domestic investment. The correct equality is: private saving equals gross private domestic investment plus net foreign investment plus the government budget deficit. Gross private saving in 1993 was $1,002 billion while gross private domestic investment was only $882 billion. Thus, even in the aggregate, the taxes on the saving out of wage income are not fully canceled by the full deductibility of investment in the business tax. And it is hardly clear that any individual will recognize that he can save taxes on his wages by saving instead of consuming. He may well recognize that the choice is between paying a consumption tax now and saving and paying a consumption tax later.

The business tax also turns out to be largely a consumption tax. Hall and Rabushka declare, "Fundamentally, people pay taxes, not businesses."[4] They elaborate in the updated version of their book: "Remember, businesses don't pay taxes, only individuals do. And, higher taxes on business are borne in part by the employees in fewer jobs and lower wages."[5] Then, "Remember, the true incidence or burden of income taxes on corporations is not fully known—some is effectively paid by owners, some by employees, and some by consumers (who are workers in another guise)."[6]

The true incidence of taxes on all business combined, corporate and noncorporate, essentially all market production, however, must be clear. Like all other costs, these taxes must be reflected in the prices of business products. This need be qualified only to the extent that taxes on market production induce a substitution of nonmarket production or leisure. It is hard to believe that this qualification can amount to much in our economy.[7] It may well be argued that current business taxes, both corporate and noncorporate, are essentially a consumption tax. To the major extent that H-R-A would add to business taxation, while making business investment fully tax-deductible, they will be converting a significant part of our income tax to a consumption tax or what is, in effect, a sales tax. Its ultimate incidence on individuals will then depend upon individuals' consumption, or purchases of goods and services subject to the tax.

How Fair Is the Hall-Rabushka-Armey Proposal?

We may begin our analysis of fairness by recalling the Haig-Hicks-Simon concept of income as that which can be consumed while keeping real wealth intact.[8] This implies, it will be noted, that real capital gains, that is, those in excess of general inflation, are part of income. Some wealth has been garnered not in ordinary income subject to income taxation but in essentially untaxed capital gains.

We may next question whether consumption, and certainly the more restrictive measure of consumption taxed by H-R-A, is the sole test of individual welfare. An old joke runs, "I have been poor and I have been rich, and rich is better." And it is better not merely because the rich can enjoy higher lifetime consumption than the poor. Riches convey prestige and power and the ability to add to future income for oneself and one's children. Income and wealth also permit the acquisition of property—houses, mansions, and country homes—which produce nonmarket, untaxed consumption services. And they permit travel and untaxed consumption in foreign countries.

Income and wealth can offer security. Assuming the marginal utility of consumption is declining, there is a clear advantage to its smoothing. That is a luxury freely available to the rich and those of high incomes. With obviously imperfect financial markets for human capital, low-wage earners suffer painful losses of welfare when their earnings fluctuate downward, losses that are not fully recouped by subsequent upturns.

Calculation of the Wage Tax by Income Class

We shall focus first on the effect of H-R-A on the distribution of taxes by size of income. Measuring the distribution of the wage tax would be fairly straightforward if we had comprehensive measures of income by size class. IRS publications in the *Statistics of Income* report on components of income included in "total income" and "adjusted gross income" and on various deductions. Total income, however, excludes nontaxable interest income and the nontaxable portions of individual retirement account (IRA) distributions, pensions, and social security benefits and includes only realized (nominal) capital gains. The adjustments to get to adjusted gross income include subtraction of IRA deductions, moving expenses, one-half of the self-employment tax, self-employed health insurance deductions, Keogh retirement plan and self-employed deductions, and penalties on early withdrawal of savings and alimony paid. IRS *Statistics of Income* tables are drawn upon in our tables 3–1 through 3–7 to present estimates of total income, adjusted gross income, and various components of income, individually and combined.

In estimating the distribution of the wage tax by income class, I worked with *Statistics of Income* early tax estimates for 1993, the year used by Hall and Rabushka in their estimates. I first normalized "wages," that is, the income subject to "wage" taxation, actually wages and salaries, pensions, and retirement benefits, so that their total matched the Hall and Rabushka total of $3,100 billion. I then calculated the total dollar amount of the Hall and Rabushka personal allowances based on their specifications: $16,500 for married joint filers, $9,500 for single filers, $14,000 for single heads of households, and $4,500 for each dependent. I normalized these to fit the Hall and Rabushka total "family allowances" of $1,705 billion. I then subtracted the sum of these allowances, for each adjusted gross income (AGI) class, from the corresponding sum of wages. For the lower AGI classes, under $10,000 and $10,000 to $20,000, the allowances exceeded the total income subject to taxes. For each AGI class where the sum of wages minus allowances (or W minus E, for "exemptions") was negative, I put the figure at zero and renormalized to reach the Hall and Rabushka total of

49

TABLE 3–1: ADJUSTED GROSS INCOME, SELECTED COMPONENTS
OF INCOME, AND INDIVIDUAL INCOME TAXES BY AGI CLASS, 1991
(billions of dollars)

AGI Class (thousands of dollars)	Adjusted Gross Income	Salaries and Wages	Taxable Interest	Nontaxable Interest
Less than 10	102.6	123.0	20.0	2.0
10–under 20	373.2	280.6	29.2	1.5
20–under 30	433.3	350.0	22.5	2.5
30–under 40	429.1	354.1	21.0	2.6
40–under 50	393.5	327.2	16.8	2.8
50–under 75	685.6	573.6	27.3	5.9
75–under 100	305.0	243.5	14.6	3.8
100–under 200	339.1	233.6	20.6	7.3
200–under 500	196.3	111.6	15.2	6.8
500–under 1,000	79.6	39.0	7.4	3.2
1,000 and over	127.1	38.0	14.7	4.7
All incomes	3,464.5	2,674.3	209.4	43.1

AGI Class (thousands of dollars)	Dividends	Net Capital Gains	Pensions and Annuities	Total Income Tax
Less than 10	4.2	7.9	14.5	0.6
10–under 20	5.8	2.9	38.4	20.4
20–under 30	5.8	3.9	36.4	38.5
30–under 40	5.8	3.6	30.6	46.0
40–under 50	4.9	3.8	26.3	43.0
50–under 75	11.0	9.7	42.2	88.6
75–under 100	6.2	6.9	17.3	47.3
100–under 200	11.3	15.9	19.4	62.8
200–under 500	8.7	16.7	9.5	46.8
500–under 1,000	4.4	9.9	2.9	20.9
1,000 and over	9.2	29.2	1.8	33.7
All incomes	77.3	110.2	239.2	448.4

SOURCE: Internal Revenue Service, *Statistics of Income.*

TABLE 3–2: ADJUSTED GROSS INCOME, SELECTED COMPONENTS OF INCOME, AND INDIVIDUAL INCOME TAXES, AS PERCENTAGES OF ADJUSTED GROSS INCOME, BY AGI CLASS, 1991
(percent)

AGI Class (thousands of dollars)	Salaries and Wages	Taxable Interest	Dividends	Nontaxable Interest
Less than 10	119.80	19.52	2.23	1.91
10–under 20	75.19	7.83	1.55	0.40
20–under 30	80.77	5.20	1.33	0.58
30–under 40	82.53	4.89	1.36	0.61
40–under 50	83.14	4.28	1.25	0.70
50–under 75	83.66	3.98	1.60	0.86
75–under 100	79.84	4.79	2.03	1.24
100–under 200	68.89	6.08	3.34	2.16
200–under 500	56.85	7.74	4.45	3.47
500–under 1,000	49.03	9.32	5.50	4.05
1,000 and over	29.93	11.58	7.24	3.70
All incomes	77.19	6.04	2.23	1.24

AGI Class (thousands of dollars)	Net Capital Gains	Pensions and Annuities	Total Income Tax
Less than 10	4.12	114.24	1,040.39
10–under 20	0.77	10.29	5.48
20–under 30	0.89	8.41	8.88
30–under 40	0.85	7.13	10.71
40–under 50	0.96	6.68	10.92
50–under 75	1.41	6.16	12.92
75–under 100	2.25	5.67	15.50
100–under 200	4.68	5.73	18.53
200–under 500	8.50	4.82	23.83
500–under 1,000	12.45	3.67	26.27
1,000 and over	22.95	1.41	26.47
All incomes	3.18	6.91	12.94

SOURCE: Internal Revenue Service, *Statistics of Income.*

TABLE 3–3
TOTAL INCOME, ADJUSTED GROSS INCOME, SELECTED COMPO-
NENTS OF INCOME, AND INDIVIDUAL INCOME TAXES, BY AGI
CLASS, BASED ON SAMPLE OF EARLY TAX RETURNS, 1993
(billions of dollars)

AGI Class (thousands of dollars)	Total Income (or Loss)	Adjusted Gross Income	Salaries and Wages	Taxable Interest
Less than 10	130.6	128.7	113.4	11.0
10–under 20	342.5	339.9	257.6	17.6
20–under 30	400.3	397.0	324.7	10.7
30–under 40	396.6	393.7	337.4	8.5
40–under 50	368.9	367.0	308.0	10.3
50–under 75	671.0	666.7	565.4	14.5
75–under 100	332.0	330.5	281.5	7.3
100–under 200	362.2	357.4	256.4	12.5
200 and over	354.2	346.9	190.9	28.5
All incomes	3,358.3	3,327.8	2,635.3	120.8

AGI Class (thousands of dollars)	Dividends	Net Capital Gains	Pensions and Annuities	Total Income Tax
Less than 10	3.5	2.3	13.3	2.9
10–under 20	5.6	2.6	36.6	16.6
20–under 30	5.3	3.9	35.9	33.0
30–under 40	4.8	3.4	24.8	40.0
40–under 50	5.7	4.8	29.6	39.6
50–under 75	9.7	12.3	44.1	82.7
75–under 100	5.8	6.7	15.3	49.8
100–under 200	10.7	14.7	19.2	66.0
200 and over	25.7	34.0	10.0	97.7
All incomes	76.7	84.8	228.9	428.3

SOURCE: Internal Revenue Service, *Statistics of Income.*

TABLE 3–4
Total Income, Adjusted Gross Income, Selected Components of Income, and Individual Income Taxes as Percentages of Total Income, by AGI Class, Based on Sample of
Early Tax Returns, 1993
(percent)

AGI Class (thousands of dollars)	Salaries and Wages	Taxable Interest	Dividends
Less than 10	86.81	8.38	2.69
10–under 20	75.20	5.13	1.63
20–under 30	81.12	2.68	1.33
30–under 40	85.06	2.13	1.20
40–under 50	83.50	2.79	1.54
50–under 75	84.26	2.17	1.44
75–under 100	84.79	2.20	1.75
100–under 200	70.80	3.44	2.95
200 and over	53.89	8.05	7.25
All incomes	78.47	3.60	2.28

AGI Class (thousands of dollars)	Net Capital Gains	Pensions and Annuities	Total Income Tax
Less than 10	1.79	10.18	2.22
10–under 20	0.77	10.69	4.85
20–under 30	0.98	8.98	8.23
30–under 40	0.87	6.25	10.09
40–under 50	1.29	8.03	10.73
50–under 75	1.84	6.57	12.32
75–under 100	2.01	4.61	15.00
100–under 200	4.07	5.31	18.24
200 and over	9.60	2.82	27.60
All incomes	2.53	6.82	12.75

Source: Internal Revenue Service, *Statistics of Income.*

TABLE 3–5
WAGES, SALARIES, PENSIONS, AND ANNUITIES, ALL OTHER INCOME, AND CAPITAL INCOME, BY AGI CLASS, AS PERCENTAGES OF ADJUSTED GROSS INCOME, 1991
(percent)

AGI Class (thousands of dollars)	Adjusted Gross Income (in billions of dollars)	Wages, Salaries, Pensions, and Annuities	All Other Income	Capital Income
Less than 10	102.6	133.9	(33.88)	33.17
10–under 20	373.2	85.5	14.52	10.55
20–under 30	433.3	89.2	10.82	8.00
30–under 40	429.1	89.7	10.34	7.71
40–under 50	393.5	89.8	10.18	7.19
50–under 75	685.6	89.8	10.19	7.85
75–under 100	305.0	85.5	14.50	10.30
100–under 200	339.1	74.6	25.38	16.26
200–under 500	196.3	61.7	38.33	24.17
500–under 1,000	79.6	52.7	47.30	31.33
1,000 and over	127.1	31.3	68.66	45.48
All incomes	3,464.5	84.10	15.90	12.70

SOURCE: Internal Revenue Service, *Statistics of Income.*

$1,705 billion, shown in table 3–8. I then subtracted the normalized vector of allowances from the normalized vector of wages and thus generated a normalized wage tax base base vector with a sum equal to the Hall and Rabushka wage tax base of $1,395 billion. This normalized wage tax vector in turn, at the Hall and Rabushka flat rate of 19 percent, gave a wage *tax* vector with a total wage tax equal to their $265 billion (or, precisely, $265.05 billion), shown in table 3–9.

I then took the total income tax (of $428.299 billion) reported in the early returns, shown in table 3–3, and normalized this distribution by AGI class to fit a total of $508.62 billion later reported, very close to the $510 billion indi-

TABLE 3–6

WAGES, SALARIES, PENSIONS, AND ANNUITIES, ALL OTHER INCOME,
AND CAPITAL INCOME, BY AGI CLASS, AS PERCENTAGES OF TOTAL
INCOME, BASED ON SAMPLE OF EARLY TAX RETURNS, 1993
(percent)

AGI Class (thousands of dollars)	Total Income or Loss (billions of dollars)	Wages, Salaries, Pensions, and Annuities	All Other Income	Capital Income
Less than 10	130.6	96.99	3.01	12.87
10–under 20	342.5	85.89	14.11	7.53
20–under 30	400.3	90.10	9.90	5.00
30–under 40	396.6	91.31	8.69	4.20
40–under 50	368.9	91.53	8.47	5.62
50–under 75	671.0	90.83	9.17	5.44
75–under 100	332.0	89.40	10.60	5.96
100–under 200	362.2	76.11	23.89	10.46
200 and over	354.2	56.71	43.29	24.90
All incomes	3,358.3	85.29	14.71	8.41

SOURCE: Internal Revenue Service, *Statistics of Income.*

cated by Hall and Rabushka. I next normalized "total income," as defined by the IRS and reported in the *Statistics of Income* early returns, by multiplying the total income distribution by the ratio of 508.62/428.299, so that the total income series, shown in table 3–8, corresponded to the taxes paid. I was then able to compare all taxes, current and under the Hall-Rabushka and Armey proposal, as percentages of total income. For Hall and Rabushka, then, the incidence of the wage tax is simply, for each AGI class, the wage tax as calculated above, divided by total income.

The total business tax for Hall and Rabushka is 19 percent of their business tax base of $1,903 billion. Accepting their figure indicates a business tax revenue of $361.57 billion (they put it at $362 billion) and a total actual revenue of $626.62 billion (as against their published figure of $627 billion).

TABLE 3–7
MEAN TOTAL INCOME AND MEAN INCOME IN WAGES, SALARIES, AND PENSIONS, BY AGI CLASS, BASED ON SAMPLE OF EARLY TAX RETURNS, 1993
(dollars)

AGI Class (thousands of dollars)	Mean Total Income	Mean Wages, Salaries, and Pensions
Less than 5	2,520	2,278
5–under 10	7,564	6,215
10–under 15	12,547	10,555
15–under 20	17,501	15,298
20–under 25	22,600	20,054
25–under 30	27,562	25,199
30–under 40	34,995	31,955
40–under 50	44,838	41,040
50–under 75	60,883	55,302
75–under 100	85,650	76,570
100–under 200	132,616	100,937
200 and over	431,944	244,967
All incomes	31,454	26,826

SOURCE: Internal Revenue Service, *Statistics of Income.*

I then calculated the Armey wage tax by substituting the larger Armey exemptions, or "standard deductions" as the Armey proposal calls them. These are, as specified in H.R. 4585, $24,700 for a joint return, $16,200 for a "head of household," $12,350 for an individual, and $5,000 for each dependent. Normalizing these consistently with the methods applied to Hall and Rabushka, I calculated the Armey sums of wages minus exemptions (W-E), again zeroing out those classes where ΣW minus $\Sigma E < 0$. The Armey exemptions came to $2,263.172 billion, or $558.172 billion more than the Hall and Rabushka exemptions, both shown in table 3–8. The Armey wage tax base was thus reduced precisely to $836.828 billion, $558.172 billion less than the Hall and Rabushka wage base.

TABLE 3–8
TOTAL INCOME AND WAGES, SALARIES, AND PENSIONS, HALL AND
RABUSHKA AND ARMEY APPLICABLE EXEMPTIONS AND WAGE
BASES, BY AGI CLASS, BASED ON SAMPLE OF EARLY TAX
RETURNS, 1993
(billions of dollars)

AGI Class (thousands of dollars)	Total Income[a]	Wages, Salaries,[b] and Pensions	Applicable Exemptions[c]		Wage Bases	
			H-R	Armey	H-R	Armey
Less than 10	155.1	137.1	137.1	137.1	0	0
10–under 20	406.8	318.4	318.4	318.4	0	0
20–under 30	475.3	390.3	277.9	357.5	112.4	32.9
30–under 40	471.0	392.0	227.9	310.8	164.1	81.2
40–under 50	438.1	365.4	189.3	268.2	176.1	97.2
50–under 75	796.8	659.7	293.5	434.9	366.2	224.7
75–under 100	394.2	321.2	117.7	186.2	203.5	135.0
100–under 200	430.1	298.4	94.6	157.0	203.8	141.3
200 and over	420.6	217.4	48.6	92.9	168.9	124.5
All incomes	3,988.1	3,100.0	1,705.0	2,263.2	1,395.0	836.8

a. Adjusted to match income tax of $508.62 billion.
b. Adjusted to match total of $3,100 billion.
c. Distributed among AGI classes where exemptions do not exceed wages.
SOURCE: Internal Revenue Service, *Statistics of Income.*

I was then able to calculate the Armey flat tax rate, r, that would generate, or would have generated in 1993, the same total revenue as Hall and Rabushka and, if their calculations were correct, as current law. This entailed simply solving for r the equation:

$TT = r * (BTB + AWTB)$, where TT = total taxes, BTB = business tax base, and $AWTB$ = Armey wage tax base. Substituting the actual numbers, we have:

$626.62 = r * (1903 + 836.828)$, whence $r = 0.228707787$ or 22.87 percent.

Multiplying this by the Armey tax base vector (by AGI

TABLE 3–9

PERSONAL INCOME TAX AND HALL AND RABUSHKA AND ARMEY
WAGE TAXES, BY AGI CLASS, BASED ON SAMPLE OF EARLY TAX
RETURNS, 1993

(billions of dollars)

AGI Class (thousands of dollars)	Personal Income Tax[a]	Wage Taxes	
		Hall-Rabushka[b]	Armey [c]
Less than 10	3.4	0	0
10–under 20	19.7	0	0
20–under 30	39.1	21.4	7.5
30–under 40	47.5	31.2	18.6
40–under 50	47.0	33.5	22.2
50–under 75	98.2	69.6	51.4
75–under 100	59.1	38.7	30.9
100–under 200	78.4	38.7	32.3
200 and over	116.1	32.1	28.5
All incomes	508.6	265.1	191.4

a. Adjusted to $508.62 billion.
b. At 19 percent.
c. At 22.87 percent.
SOURCE: Internal Revenue Service, *Statistics of Income.*

class) generates the Armey wage tax, which comes to a total of $191.389 billion (table 3–9). This is considerably less than the Hall and Rabushka wage tax of $265.05 billion we have noted above. The Armey business tax, conversely, will be correspondingly more than the Hall and Rabushka business tax of $361.569 billion, actually coming to $435.23 billion, as seen in table 3–10.

The wage tax in itself will generally tax most taxpayers less than they pay currently in individual income taxes, which include large amounts of noncorporate business taxes, as well as taxes on capital income. The distributional implications of substituting a wage tax for an income tax may be anticipated by comparing, by AGI class, the ratios

TABLE 3–10
BUSINESS TAXES: CURRENT AND HALL AND RABUSHKA AND
ARMEY FLAT TAXES, BY AGI CLASS, BASED ON SAMPLE OF EARLY
TAX RETURNS, 1993
(billions of dollars)

AGI Class (thousands of dollars)	Current Business Tax	Flat-Tax Business Taxes	
		Hall-Rabushka[a]	Armey[b]
Less than 10	31.4	47.9	57.7
10–under 20	26.3	40.1	48.3
20–under 30	29.3	44.7	53.9
30–under 40	27.8	42.4	51.0
40–under 50	25.5	38.9	46.8
50–under 75	43.0	65.6	79.0
75–under 100	20.0	30.5	36.7
100–under 200	20.2	30.7	37.0
200 and over	13.6	20.7	24.9
All incomes	237.1	361.6	435.2

a. At 19 percent.
b. At 22.87 percent.
SOURCE: Internal Revenue Service, *Statistics of Income.*

to total income of various of its components. In 1991, salaries and wages plus pensions averaged some 90 percent of
AGI for those with income between $20,000 and $75,000,
as shown in table 3–5, and 31 percent for those with AGIs
of $1,000,000 or over. By contrast, capital income—inter-
est, dividends, and capital gains—all excluded from taxation by H-R-A, averaged no more than 8 percent of AGI for
the classes from $20,000 to $75,000 but was 45 percent of
AGI for the $1,000,000 and over group.

Of major importance with relation to size distribution is the failure to include all real, accrued capital gains,
which are concentrated overwhelmingly among the very
highest income classes. A small indication of the significance of this concentration is found in the published data
for realized capital gains. In 1991, "net capital gains" con-

TABLE 3–11
CURRENT INCOME AND BUSINESS TAXES, AS PERCENTAGE OF
TOTAL INCOME, BY AGI CLASS, 1993
(percent)

AGI Class (thousands of dollars)	Personal Income Tax	Nonbusiness Portion of Personal Income Tax	Current Business Tax	Current Total Tax
Less than 10	2.22	1.70	20.25	21.95
10–under 20	4.85	3.71	6.47	10.18
20–under 30	8.23	6.30	6.17	12.48
30–under 40	10.09	7.73	5.90	13.62
40–under 50	10.73	8.22	5.82	14.04
50–under 75	12.32	9.44	5.40	14.83
75–under 100	15.00	11.49	5.07	16.56
100–under 200	18.24	13.97	4.69	18.65
200 and over	27.60	21.13	3.22	24.36
All incomes	12.75	9.77	5.95	15.71

SOURCE: Internal Revenue Service, *Statistics of Income.*

stituted 22.95 percent of adjusted gross incomes of $1,000,000 or more, as shown in table 3–2. They constituted less than 1 percent of adjusted gross incomes in the $10,000 to $50,000 classes.

Those in the $30,000 to $40,000 class paid taxes equal to 10.1 percent of AGI according to the *Statistics of Income* sample of early returns for 1993, as shown in table 3–11. Taxpayers in that class with a family of four and the mean wage and pension income of those in that class, $31,955 as shown in table 3–7, would pay no wage tax under the Armey plan. My estimate of Armey wage taxes that would be paid by all in the $30,000 to $40,000 AGI class, is 3.94 percent of total income, shown in table 3–12. For the $50,000 to $75,000 AGI class, the average wage tax that would be paid under the Armey flat tax would be 6.45

TABLE 3–12
ARMEY FLAT TAX: WAGE AND BUSINESS TAXES, AS PERCENTAGE
OF TOTAL INCOME, BY AGI CLASS, 1993
(percent)

AGI Class (thousands of dollars)	Wage Tax	Business Tax	Total Tax
Less than 10	0.00	37.18	37.18
10–under 20	0.00	11.88	11.88
20–under 30	1.58	11.33	12.91
30–under 40	3.94	10.83	14.77
40–under 50	5.08	10.68	15.76
50–under 75	6.45	9.91	16.36
75–under 100	7.83	9.31	17.14
100–under 200	7.51	8.60	16.12
200 and over	6.77	5.92	12.69
All incomes	4.80	10.91	15.71

SOURCE: Internal Revenue Service, *Statistics of Income.*

percent of income. Personal income taxes for this group, based on 1993 early returns, were 12.32 percent of total income (table 3–11). In 1991, individual income taxes in this AGI class came to 12.9 percent of AGI, as shown in table 3–2.

The $1,000,000 and over class, in 1991, paid taxes that came to 26.47 percent. At the 22.87 percent flat rate, since their wage, salary, and pension income was only 31.34 percent of AGI, they would have paid "flat" taxes equal to 7.17 percent of AGI, or slightly less, depending on the number of their exemptions. The H-R-A wage taxes are smaller proportions of income than the current individual income tax at all income levels, as may be seen by comparing figures in table 3–11 with tables 3–12 and 3–13. But while progressive with respect to wage income, because of

61

TABLE 3–13

HALL AND RABUSHKA FLAT TAX: WAGE AND BUSINESS TAXES, AS
PERCENTAGE OF TOTAL INCOME, BY AGI CLASS, 1993

(percent)

AGI Class (thousands of dollars)	Wage Tax	Business Tax	Total Tax
Less than 10	0.00	30.89	30.89
10–under 20	0.00	9.87	9.87
20–under 30	4.49	9.41	13.91
30–under 40	6.62	9.00	15.62
40–under 50	7.64	8.87	16.51
50–under 75	8.73	8.23	16.97
75–under 100	9.81	7.73	17.54
100–under 200	9.00	7.15	16.15
200 and over	7.63	4.92	12.55
All incomes	6.65	9.07	15.71

SOURCE: Internal Revenue Service, *Statistics of Income.*

the personal deductions, it is regressive at higher income
levels with respect to total income.

Calculation of the Business Tax by Income Class

The distribution of tax by income class depends much
more with H-R-A, however, on the incidence of the business tax on consumption. If we can specify the parameters
of the consumption relation we can calculate the consumption of the taxpayers in each AGI class.

To get an initial handle on this, we might make some
simplifying assumption. The most simple, consistent with
Milton Friedman's permanent income hypothesis or
Franco Modigliani's life-cycle hypothesis in its extreme
form with no bequests, would be that consumption is the
same proportion of income in all income classes. I was an
early defender of the permanent income hypothesis,[9] but

TABLE 3–14
"BURDENS" OF 5 PERCENT CONSUMPTION TAX, AS PERCENTAGE
OF "EXPANDED INCOME," ADJUSTED GROSS INCOME, AND TOTAL
INCOME, FROM JOINT COMMITTEE ON TAXATION, BASED ON
SAMPLE OF EARLY TAX RETURNS, 1993
(percent)

Size of AGI (thousands of dollars)	Burden as % of "Expanded Income"	AGI as % of "Expanded Income"	Burden as % of AGI	Burden as % of Total Income[a]
Less than 10	3.70	30.40	12.17	12.06
10–under 20	2.66	68.90	3.86	3.83
20–under 30	2.90	78.70	3.68	3.65
30–under 40	2.92	83.00	3.52	3.49
40–under 50	2.94	84.90	3.46	3.44
50–under 75	2.77	86.10	3.22	3.20
75–under 100	2.63	87.20	3.02	3.00
100–under 200	2.50	88.90	2.81	2.78
200 and over	1.76	90.30	1.95	1.91

a. Percentages of total income calculated by multiplying percentages of AGI by ratios of AGI to total income indicated in *Statistics of Income* sample of 1993 early returns.
SOURCE: Internal Revenue Service, *Statistics of Income;* and Joint Committee on Taxation.

surely a more realistic and relevant assumption here, recognizing that neither AGI nor taxable income is permanent income, would be that consumption is a declining proportion of income as income rises. This is clearly true, not only for observations of a single year, where transitory components of income may generate a flatter consumption-income relation, but for long-term averages that would show smaller proportions of transitory income. Higher-income groups do live longer and save more for retirement and do leave proportionately more in their estates, a phenomenon likely to become more prominent because

TABLE 3–15
TOTAL TAXES: CURRENT INDIVIDUAL AND CORPORATE INCOME
TAXES AND HALL AND RABUSHKA AND ARMEY FLAT TAXES, BY
AGI CLASS, BASED ON SAMPLE OF EARLY TAX RETURNS, 1993
(billions of dollars)

| AGI Class (thousands of dollars) | Current Total Tax | Flat-Tax Total Taxes | |
		Hall and Rabushka[a]	Armey[b]
Less than 10	34.1	47.9	57.7
10–under 20	41.4	40.1	48.3
20–under 30	59.3	66.1	61.4
30–under 40	64.2	73.6	69.6
40–under 50	61.5	72.3	69.0
50–under 75	118.2	135.2	130.4
75–under 100	65.3	69.2	67.6
100–under 200	80.2	69.5	69.3
200 and over	102.5	52.8	53.4
All incomes	626.6	626.6	626.6

a. At 19 percent.
b. At 22.87 percent.
SOURCE: Internal Revenue Service, *Statistics of Income.*

of the elimination (at least in Hall and Rabushka) of inheritance taxes. And they travel more and spend less of
their incomes on the domestic consumption that would
be subject to the H-R-A business taxes.

Assuming that all the business taxes of H-R-A are
passed on in higher prices,[10] we can calculate how much is
paid by each income class by distributing the total business tax in proportion to the consumption of each class. I
have calculated the distribution of the H-R-A business taxes
as a percentage of total income from estimates prepared
by the staff of the Joint Committee on Taxation. The JCT
reported using saving rates derived from the Survey of

TABLE 3–16
CURRENT AND FLAT TAXES AS PERCENTAGE OF TOTAL INCOME, BY
AGI CLASS, 1993
(percent)

AGI Class (thousands of dollars)	Current Total Tax	Hall and Rabushka Total Tax	Armey Total Tax
Less than 10	21.95	30.89	37.18
10–under 20	10.18	9.87	11.88
20–under 30	12.48	13.91	12.91
30–under 40	13.62	15.62	14.77
40–under 50	14.04	16.51	15.76
50–under 75	14.83	16.97	16.36
75–under 100	16.56	17.54	17.14
100–under 200	18.65	16.15	16.12
200 and over	24.36	12.55	12.69
All incomes	15.71	15.71	15.71

SOURCE: Tables 3–13, 3–14 and 3–15.

Consumer Finances to impute consumption by income group. The staff then calculated the "burden" of a 5 percent consumption tax as percentages of their measure of "extended income" by AGI class.[11]

I was able to use *Statistics of Income* data on total income and AGI to convert the "burdens" into percentages of total income, as shown in Table 3–14. I multiplied these percentages by the total income vector (table 3–8) and normalized the resulting vector so that it summed to the Hall and Rabushka business tax total taxable income of $1,903 billion. I had only to multiply this vector by the Hall and Rabushka flat tax rate of 19 percent to get the business tax by AGI class and its sum of $361.57 billion (table 3–10). I then divided this business tax vector by total income to get the tax as a percentage of total income, or the vector of Hall and Rabushka business tax effective rates, shown in table 3–13.

Since the Armey business tax had the same base but differed only in the tax rate applied, the Armey business tax and effective rates were calculated simply by multiplying the corresponding Hall and Rabushka numbers by the ratio, 0.2287077875/0.19. The resulting Armey business tax vector is shown in table 3–10. Similarly, we can prepare a distribution of business income taxes under current law; I have assumed that the income taxes not related to business under current law are distributed in the same fashion as total income taxes. We take the total business income tax under current law in 1993 to be the corporate income taxes of $118 billion reported by Hall and Rabushka and the portion of individual income taxes related to business income, which I estimate, on the basis of information from the *Statistics of Income* staff, at $119.1 billion. The total then is $237.1 billion. To calculate the business tax vector under current law, we merely scale down the Hall and Rabushka business tax vector by the ratio 237.1/361.57; the resulting current business tax vector is also found in table 3–10. The current-law, nonbusiness individual income taxes to be distributed are $508.62 billion minus $119.1 billion, or $389.52 billion. The total tax vectors for current law and the two versions of the flat tax are shown in table 3–15.

We thus have all the ingredients for a comparison of wage, business, and total taxes for Hall and Rabushka and for Armey with the personal income tax and the totals of nonbusiness income tax and business tax under current law.

Distribution of the Wage and Business Taxes Combined

We may note first in table 3–11 the effective rates of taxation under current law. Looking at the personal income tax alone, we see that is clearly progressive, rising from 2.22 percent and 4.85 percent for the lowest AGI classes, under $20,000, to 18.24 percent and 27.60 percent for the $100,000 to $200,000 and the $200,000 and over classes.

The business tax (as with Hall-Rabushka and Armey) is, however, highly regressive. Even apart from the very high effective rate of 20.25 percent for the under $10,000 group,[12] effective rates decline from 6.47 percent for the $10,000 to $20,000 AGI class to 3.22 percent for the $200,000 and over class. This decline in the effective rates, as income rises, stems from the negative relation between measured income and the ratios of measured consumption to income, with the drop in that ratio becoming precipitous for the very wealthy.

This regressive business tax contributes to a current total tax that is less progressive than the personal income tax itself. But since the business tax is a relatively small proportion of total income under current law—5.95 percent as against 9.77 percent for the nonbusiness portion of the personal income tax—the current total tax remains generally progressive. Ignoring the lowest AGI class, we find the effective tax rate as a percentage of total income rising from 10.18 percent for the $10,000 to $20,000 AGI class to 18.65 percent and 24.36 percent for the two highest classes, as shown in table 3–14.

When we turn to the Hall and Rabushka flat tax, shown in table 3–13, we see a very different picture. First, much of the Hall and Rabushka tax burden has been shifted from the individual income tax to the highly regressive business tax. The overall proportions now are 9.07 percent of income for the business tax and only 6.65 percent of income for the wage tax. Second, despite its large personal allowances or exemptions, the wage tax itself, with its flat rate and exclusion of all taxation of income interest, dividends, and capital gains, which are received overwhelmingly by upper-income groups, is much less progressive than the current income tax.

The Hall and Rabushka wage tax rate rises from zero to those under $20,000 (undoubtedly not quite right because of my method of estimating from aggregates within classes; there were certainly some taxpayers without dependents who were paying taxes) to 4.49 percent for the $20,000 to $30,000 group and ultimately to a high of 9.81 percent for the $75,000 to $100,000 AGI class. It then declines to 9.00 percent for the $100,000 to $200,000 class and to 7.63 percent for the $200,000 and over class. It is the steady progression of the tax percentages up to $100,000 that is the basis for the repeated assertions by Hall and Rabushka that their proposed flat tax is progressive.

In so claiming, however, they ignore the very regressive nature of their business tax, which is now a considerably larger component of total taxation. They have in effect moved one step in the direction of more progressivity by sharply raising their personal allowances from the current law exemptions,[13] but three steps away from progressivity, with the substitution in effect of a regressive sales tax for much of the current income tax, the exclusion from the individual tax of the capital income earned chiefly by upper-income groups, and the abandonment of a progressive rate structure. The Hall and Rabushka total tax effective rates, after the very high 30.89 percent for the under $10,000 group, move from 9.87 percent for the $10,000 to $20,000 class and 13.91 percent for the $20,000 to $30,000 class, to 17.54 percent for the $75,000 to $100,000 class. For the highest income classes, though, the Hall and Rabushka plan turns sharply regressive. The share of total income taxed falls to 16.15 percent for the $100,000 to $200,000 class and to 12.55 percent for the $200,000 and over class.

The pattern for the Armey version of the flat tax, shown in table 3–12, can now be explained. The Armey tax would shift even more of taxation to business taxes, which reach 10.91 percent of total income, reducing the wage tax proportion to 4.80 percent. With its considerably higher exemptions, the Armey wage tax is thus more progressive, although still turning regressive for incomes over $100,000. But the larger business tax contributes to Armey total tax effective rates that are more regressive than the Hall and Rabushka version. In the two lowest AGI classes, essentially free of the wage tax because of the high exemptions (and presumed to pay no wage tax in our calculations), the Armey effective rates are much higher than Hall and Rabushka, 37.18 percent against 30.89 percent and 11.88 percent against 9.87 percent. The Armey bill would collect $106 billion from taxpayers in these two classes, $18 billion more than the $88 billion collected by Hall and Rabushka, as seen in table 3–15. But it then takes less from the AGI classes between $20,000 and $100,000.

Table 3–16 offers a recapitulation of the figures for total taxes. By construction, all generate the same total of 15.71 percent of total income. Ignoring the under $10,000 income class, we see that the current income tax system is progressive over all classes.[14] Hall and Rabushka taxes would be considerably higher than current taxes for all the income groups between $20,000 and $100,000, essentially the much-mentioned "middle class." They would then be much lower for the highest income groups: 16.15 percent of total income as against 18.65 percent for the $100,000 to $200,000 class and 12.55 percent compared with 24.36 percent for the $200,000 and over class. The Armey flat tax version would also have considerably higher taxes than current law for the middle-income classes, although somewhat less than the Hall and Rabushka flat tax. For the $200,000 and over class, the Armey total tax would be 12.69 percent of total income as against the Hall and Rabushka 12.55 percent, both little more than half the current total tax figure of 24.36 percent.[15, 16]

I of course cannot claim complete accuracy for most of these figures. The flat tax calculations begin with the Hall and Rabushka base of aggregates. And my aggregation within AGI classes, made necessary by the unavailability to me of individual taxpayer data relating exemptions to total income, introduces some error into the results. Working with data from a sample of early 1993 returns introduces some further error to the extent that early returns, while an overwhelming proportion of the total, are not fully representative. It is hard to believe, however, that corrections of any of these errors would make much difference to the relative figures presented.

Other adjustments might make more difference, chiefly in the direction of showing current taxes and the proposed flat taxes all to be less progressive or more regressive. It would be particularly important to adjust properly for capital gains, which, as we have noted, are concentrated very much among the very highest income groups. To some extent, of course, the high incomes depend on the inclusion of these gains.

We should be including not nominal but real capital gains in our measures of income. But we should be measuring all capital gains, as they accrue, not merely those that are realized. The extent of nonrealization may be gleaned from the budget estimates of revenue losses from the step-up of basis, which eliminates capital gains passed on at death from taxation; death is inevitable but, in this instance, taxes are not. These revenue losses were put at $28.3 billion[17] for 1995, implying that capital gains of perhaps $80 billion (assuming an average tax rate of about 33.7 percent) escaped taxation by being "unrealized."

The inflation adjustment would of course cut the figures on realized and unrealized capital gains sharply, since they reflect nominal gains over sometimes long periods during which prices rose substantially. With current low rates of inflation, the generally much larger totals of all net gains, "realized" or not, would certainly be higher, as I found them to be some years ago.[18] It would be useful to have such estimates prepared on a current basis. Inclusion of all real, accrued capital gains would reveal that both the current system and H-R-A are less progressive than indicated by measures without their inclusion. Since capital gains there are not taxed at all, the adjustment would reduce the measure of progressivity more for H-R-A than it would for the current system.

The H-R-A wage tax is very progressive up to middle incomes, because of the large standard deductions, but then regressive at upper incomes as its base of salaries, wages, and pensions becomes a considerably smaller proportion of total income. But, as we have noted, by substantially increasing the business or consumption tax, H-R-A raises taxes on the very poor who pay no wage tax under H-R-A, but also pay no income tax under current law. If the earned-income tax credit is eliminated, the increased burden of H-R-A on the very poor is sharply increased. And H-R-A raises taxes substantially on the middle class, up to incomes of $100,000. Public statements and tables purporting to indicate vastly reduced individual income taxes for middle-income classes under the flat tax grievously ignore the vastly increased business taxes to be paid by consumers.

By my preference function and, I think, that of most Americans, both proposed flat taxes fail the test of vertical equity. Both rely heavily on a business tax falling on consumption; there can be no reasonable doubt that consumption taxes are regressive with respect to income. And both tax wage and pension income but exclude taxation of capital income, which is received disproportionately by the rich. Hall and Rabushka declare, "Tax reform will be a tremendous boon to the economic elite from the start."[19] My estimates clearly confirm this. And I see no reason to believe that this initial boon will not be permanent.

The current income tax does so badly by any measures of horizontal equity—that is, people with the same income paying the same tax—that one might expect that H-R-A could hardly be worse. That, unfortunately, is not the case. The H-R-A wage and pension tax leaves totally untaxed the income from interest, dividends, and capital gains. Its business tax is the same for all those with the same income who consume the same proportion of their income. Big savers pay a smaller proportion of their income on the business tax, however, and small savers pay a

71

larger proportion. Those who consume more abroad are also liable for smaller proportions of their income under the business tax.

A household earning $100,000 a year in wages or pensions would pay its full share of taxes. A household earning $100,000 a year—or more—in interest, dividends, or capital gains would pay no individual taxes at all! Both households would pay *in addition* the increased taxes on their consumption resulting from the increased business taxes.[20]

Effects on Efficiency

Let us turn from issues of fairness to those of efficiency for the economy as a whole, now and in the future. First, if often ignored in current discussions of tax policy, a consumption tax reduces the force of automatic stabilizers. It does so because consumption varies less over the business cycle than income; investment and income vary more. Hence, when the economy slows, taxes fall less with a consumption tax. Conversely, when the economy booms and investment surges, since business investment is fully deductible, tax receipts grow less than with income taxes. It might be a useful exercise to estimate how much average unemployment and average inflation would be increased by the move to consumption taxes.

In the transition, at least, one can expect a major rise in the level of prices. We have observed, above, that the switch to the proposed flat tax represents an increase in the consumption tax from 5.95 percent to 9.07 percent for Hall and Rabushka and to 10.91 percent for the Armey version. On the assumption that current business taxes are passed on in higher prices, this would suggest exogenous upward pushes of 2.94 percent or 4.68 percent to prices.[21] Such increases might of course be moderated by tighter monetary policy—at real costs to the economy in lost employment and output. But they are also likely to be amplified as the initial shocks work their way through the economy.

Second, the move to expensing all business investment, which on the basis of *Statistics of Income* tabulations we may estimate will substitute a deduction of $719 billion of investment in 1995 for $553 billion of depreciation charges, offers the greatest advantage to the most durable investment. The present value of straight-line depreciation deductions on a thirty-year $100 million plant investment at a modest 8 percent discount rate is roughly $37.5 million. For a three-year investment in equipment it would be $85.9 million. Offering expensing to both then adds about 167 percent to the present value of the tax deduction for the thirty-year investment but only 16 percent for the three-year investment.[22] It may be argued that expensing in fact is a neutral approach; no investment is taxed. But if capital income were to bear its share of the costs of government, it may better be argued that this income should be taxed as it accrues, that is, as gross income in excess of current depreciation is earned. The immediate gain by avoiding this taxation is greater for longer-lived investment.

The issue of neutrality with regard to investment is controversial and complex. I may fall back on the position of Hall and Rabushka, who assert repeatedly that their 100 percent initial write-off offers an investment "incentive."[23] The incentive then is greatest for long-lived investment. But why should there be any incentive for business investment? Why should business not be left free, without government intervention, to invest to the extent it considers profitable? It is usually argued that investment contributes to growth, but this can be true, surely, only if it adds to future product more than its cost. If government tax subsidies with a present value of $10 induce a firm to make a $100 investment that would have a payoff of $95 without subsidy, the investment would be contributing not to growth but to economic decline.

The benefit-cost principle of taxation would suggest

that taxes be associated with the social costs imposed by economic activity. A major cost of government, by way of illustration, is defense. The more capital we have, the more our economy is worth, the more we have to defend, and, we may assume, the more we will spend for defense. To exempt all capital and capital income from taxation is then to encourage the acquisition of capital beyond the point where its returns exceed or are equal to its total costs, including the costs it imposes on society and its government.

Third, H-R-A tilts the playing field against state and local investment and other expenditures by imposing a federal tax on state and local taxes. Their business tax offers no deduction for state and local taxes. These can then be expected to be passed on in higher prices to consumers who will thus be paying the state and local tax plus a 19 percent surcharge in the Hall and Rabushka formulation or a 22.87 percent surcharge in the Armey version if revenue neutrality is imposed. If we can assume that public choice has already given us an optimum amount of state and local services and taxes—which some may of course question—imposing an additional tax, which will cause total taxes to exceed the value of the services they are presumed to finance, can only discourage the provision of such services. If there is a judgment that such services are in general excessive, a judgment that I would not share, it would be in order to correct this problem up front and not with an extra federal tax.

Fourth, investment in housing would be discouraged by H-R-A in favor of other kinds of investment. Returns to owner-occupied housing in the form of imputed rent are currently not taxed while returns in the form of interest, dividends, and realized capital gains accruing as a result of other forms of investment are taxed. With the flat tax, this income from other forms of investment will now escape the individual income tax. But the flat tax, in the words of Hall, "brings the service flow of housing under the tax where the flow escapes taxation under current income tax."[24] As compared to current law, the tilt is thus clearly away from owner-occupied housing.

In addition, the elimination of tax deductibility for mortgage interest will hit housing hard. Hall and Rabushka argue that this loss will be compensated by lower before-tax interest rates. But that compensation can at best be only partial. The claim by Hall and Rabushka that the elimination of taxes on interest receipts would make lenders ready to accept lower interest rates exaggerates this possible effect in the housing market. It ignores the fact that much of current housing mortgage lending is made by financial institutions that manage their portfolios so that their net profits can be attributed to their currently tax-exempt investments. The flat tax may thus not make all that much difference in lowering before-tax interest rates to borrowers.

Hall and Rabushka also claim that their consumption tax with business investment expensing will stimulate investment. This, as they acknowledge, would increase business demand for borrowing and raise interest rates. They cannot have it both ways. If their business investment "incentive" raises business investment while owner-occupied housing preferences are eliminated, housing will surely be the loser. Indeed, Hall and Rabushka acknowledge that "improvements in the taxation of business investment would tend to draw wealth out of housing and into plant, equipment and other business investment."[25]

I am aware that it is fashionable in some circles to argue that business investment adds to productivity and provides for our future, while the current tax code, with its mortgage and property tax deductibility and nontaxation of imputable rent, biases investment toward unproductive housing. I would argue that owner-occupied housing is one of the best investments we can make in our future. It is subject to minimum obsolescence and provides the most essential services with no cyclical lows. I would suggest that investment in owner-occupied housing, in particular, has substantial externalities in encouraging nonmarket activities of home and neighborhood maintenance. I would prescribe owner-occupied housing as a substitute for many of the monstrous public rental housing projects that plague our inner cities in Chicago and elsewhere. Current housing preferences are one thing I would not discard without an adequate substitute. H-R-A eliminates the preference and tilts the playing field the other way, to business investment.

Fifth, H-R-A introduces a bias against saving in human capital. Taxation of saving in business tangible capital is presumed to be canceled by the deductibility of business investment that the saving may finance. But what about saving to finance vocational training or postsecondary education? Private household expenditures for education and training are counted as consumption.[26] If the education is provided by profit-making institutions or by state colleges or universities financed by taxes paid by business, they are subject to further taxes at the business level. The returns to such investment in education in the form of better jobs at higher salaries and wages are, however, fully taxed under H-R-A, as they are now.

I have elsewhere pointed out that business tangible investment, now at about $600 billion and 8.5 percent of GDP, is no more than perhaps 20 percent of total investment,[27] public and private, tangible and intangible. Haveman and Wolfe have recently estimated total expenditures on children at 14.5 percent of GDP, or about 12.7 percent excluding indirect, opportunity costs of mother's child care time.[28] (Opportunity costs of students' time were not included at all.) These expenditures, both by parents and government, go in considerable part to develop our vital human capital. Nondeductible private investment in education and the major government component of investment in education taxed at the federal level in H-R-A constitute more than a third of total expenditures on children. H-R-A would eliminate taxation of business tangible investment while continuing or increasing the taxation of other forms of investment.

It is curious that Hall and Rabushka, in rejecting the taxation of capital as violating a "fundamental proposition of modern public finance theory... that intermediate products should not be taxed,"[29] apparently have in mind only business capital. The product of human capital will of course be subject to their wage tax. And state and local government expenditures for education or infrastructure and anything else financed by taxes will be subject to a double tax as the H-R-A business tax, unlike current taxes, will offer no deduction against the gross business receipts necessary to pay them.

I would argue that business investment guided by the profit motive is likely without "incentives" to reach an optimum amount, as long as fiscal and monetary policy provide a full-employment environment without interest rates unduly raised by restrictive monetary policy. I see our shortages of investment in most other areas: in human capital in general and particularly in education, in basic nonmilitary research, in domestic security, and in public infrastructure. We can use more police on the beat to permit investment in a rising generation beset by crime, violence, and drugs. Incentives to business investment, while adding a surcharge to the state and local taxes necessary to finance those police, are moving in the wrong direction.

Marginal Tax Rates and Supply

Sixth, the reduction of marginal tax rates is generally seen as improving allocation between work and leisure and between consumption and saving. Not all the innovations of H-R-A are in the direction of reducing marginal rates, though. Federal income taxes are only part, and a minor part at that, of total taxes imposed on the economy. In 1993 federal personal income taxes were 9.9 percent of national income. Federal personal and corporate income taxes combined amounted to 12.3 percent of national income. Total federal tax receipts were 24.7 percent of national income, and total taxes at all levels of government came to 42.0 percent of national income. The federal taxation of state and local income taxes in the H-R-A business tax and their removal as a deduction in the wage tax add to the effective marginal rate faced by taxpayers. Similarly, the ("double") taxation of employer contributions for social security adds to the marginal tax rate on employment, presumably a further incentive to the substitution of capital for labor. We are left with that 19 percent (or 22.87 percent) federal wage tax, plus a 6.2 percent employee payroll tax for social security, plus a 1.45 percent tax for Medicare, plus business taxes of 6.2 percent on payrolls, plus business taxes on payrolls for unemployment insurance, plus a 19 percent or 22.87 percent business tax on the payroll taxes that are not deductible. Taking all these taxes into account indicates that the total marginal tax rate on wages and salaries in H-R-A will be more like 34 percent and 38 percent than the 19 or 20 or 22.87 percent we may be led to believe.[30]

I should like, however, to question the widespread tendency, found in Hall and Rabushka as elsewhere, to assume that increases in marginal return will generally increase supply. This, it would seem, entails a conclusion from substitution effects while excluding consideration of likely income effects. Take saving, for example. Are we so sure that raising the return to saving by eliminating taxation or raising interest rates will increase the rate of saving? I recall that Michael Boskin and later Lawrence Summers argued that this would happen and that Summers, at least, then changed his mind. The counterargument is that most household saving is for retirement, aimed at providing income sufficient to maintain the standard of living of one's working years. Higher returns on accumulated savings will permit greater consumption and hence generate less preretirement saving while still meeting retirement income objectives. Indeed, this argument, as I recall from my graduate student days, goes back to an article by John Cassel in the first American Economic Association volume of *Readings in Income Distribution*.

Similarly, I recall from my graduate student days articles suggesting the possibility of a "backward-bending" labor supply curve and a classic article by Lionel Robbins on the elasticity of the demand for leisure in terms of wages. Those studies suggested that higher incomes might induce less labor, not more. Clearly, leisure is a superior good, and the income effect on the demand for labor has been such that, historically, with the rise in real wages have come greatly reduced hours, shorter work weeks, longer vacations, and earlier retirement, all of course adding up to a reduction in labor supply. I would hence not share the frequently expressed confidence of Hall and Rabushka that their flat tax will generally greatly increase the supply of labor. There may be a reduced supply of labor from upper-income groups with higher aftertax earnings.[31]

Seventh, the elimination of all federal taxation of foreign earnings of U.S. residents promises greater distortions. What will happen to the wages of American residents of Detroit who cross over to work in a Windsor, Ontario, auto plant? Will their income escape U.S. taxes? This provision may significantly increase the supply of labor—to Canada. I am not one to limit the free movement of labor or capital across international borders, but the elimination of taxes on earnings of Americans from foreign investments would appear to offer undue encouragement to the movement of capital abroad. Implementation of any such net movement of capital would depend of course on creating a surplus, or reducing the deficit, on current account. Such a result would presumably follow from the fall in the value of the dollar caused by the increased supply of dollars abroad. But that increase in turn would entail a deterioration in our terms of trade with the rest of the world.

Removal of All Tax Expenditures

Aside from increased distortions that may be introduced by H-R-A, we may wish to question their removal of a number of governmental interventions, which, admittedly, have kept the economy away from what might be perfectly competitive outcomes. I have already referred to H-R-A's removal of tax preferences for owner-occupied housing—and their tilting away from such investment. In this connection, I might add special allowances for low-rent housing and tax subsidies for its construction. I share the antipathy of Hall, Rabushka, and Armey for using the tax code for "social engineering." I have always opposed tax expenditures in principle as an inefficient and deceptive form of government intervention. But it would be cavalier, cruel, and counterproductive to remove many of these expenditures without providing substitutes. Hall and Rabushka indicate awareness of this need but offer little or nothing in the way of explicit new measures to package with their flat tax. The Armey bill offers nothing at all, and one is led to believe that all deductions, exemptions, credits, and other preferences would be removed, with those people affected left to fend for themselves somehow.

One conspicuous and important example is the earned-income tax credit, estimated to come to $20.9 billion in 1995. Supplementing wages of low-income workers at a marginal rate as high as 36 percent, it is recognized as an important tool not only in reducing poverty but in increasing the supply of labor and in moving people from welfare to work. The whole current, largely means-tested welfare system, including Aid to Families with Dependent Children, food stamps, Medicaid, and low-income housing, is such that the marginal effective tax from work at the low-paying jobs that might be available to those on welfare, taking into account loss of benefits as a result of earning income, is frequently over 100 percent. The earned-income tax credit offers some remedy. Do Hall, Rabushka, and Armey mean to eliminate it, since it would clearly violate their flat tax prescription? Would they then replace it with direct payments (government spending!) outside the tax system? Or would they eliminate the means testing in the welfare system—or eliminate the whole system—to reduce effective marginal tax rates on the poor?

Fringe Benefits

Take next fringe benefits. Hall and Rabushka place them at 18 percent of compensation of employees,[32] and I will not question their estimate. The bulk of them, I presume, are for health insurance. The 1995 revenue loss to the Treasury of "exclusion of employer contributions for medical insurance premiums and medical care" was put at $60.7 billion.[33] I appreciate that fringe benefits have grown hugely over the years because of the great tax preference accorded them. The costs are deductible on corporate or other business tax returns, but, unlike wages and salaries, the benefits are not taxable to the employees. If the insurance costs were taxed, many employers and their employees would prefer to have the insurance costs paid instead in wages, with the recipients free to decide, uninfluenced by tax considerations, how much they want to spend on health care and how they want to spend it.

But this change would involve a significant drop in the total remuneration of employees. If 18 percent of the compensation of employees comes in the form of fringe benefits, replacing them with wages and salary compensation taxed at 19 percent or 22.87 percent will result in a cut of some 4 percent in employee aftertax compensation. (If the increased tax is passed on to consumers in higher prices, instead of avoided by substituting increases in wages and salaries for the fringe benefits, the costs will largely be paid for by workers in their capacity as the major consumers of the economy.)

Further, much health care might become considerably more expensive or even unavailable if no longer provided in group insurance programs at work. We already have what most Americans see as a critical problem of tens of millions without health insurance. Denying tax deductibility to all fringe benefits would almost certainly increase this number. Are the proponents of removing that deductibility ready to support and, if they are in Congress, put in place a system that will guarantee universal health insurance, or at least prevent the lost deductibility from moving us further from that goal?

Transition Dislocations

Eighth, there are enormous problems of dislocations and huge capital gains and losses intrinsic to the transition. Hall and Rabushka have paid some attention to issues of the transition, considering particularly the unused accumulated depreciation allowances and the costs of existing mortgages that lose their tax deductibility on interest, which might lead some to believe that they have been treated unfairly by a midstream change in the rules. But the problem is much greater. Hall and Rabushka point, for example, to the vastly different consequences for a relatively low-investment firm like General Motors and a rapidly growing, high-investment firm like Intel. GM's tax in 1993, if the flat tax had been in effect, would have risen from $110 million to $2.7 billion. Intel's tax would have fallen from $1.2 billion to $277 million.[34] On the assumption that competitive market conditions prevent these *relative* income changes from being passed on in price movements and assuming further that these would be permanent changes, we have at 8 percent discount rates a capital loss of $32.5 billion for GM owners and a capital gain of about $11.5 billion for those of Intel. It is conceivable that changes of this magnitude for some companies on the losing end would leave them in a position where they could not service their existing debt and could not raise new capital. They might be driven to bankruptcy, with considerable loss to their investors, to their employees, and to the economy in general. At the least, the large rents and losses resulting from the change in government tax rules may be demoralizing to investors and to the public.

The surge in prices resulting from the introduction of the flat tax would imply real losses for those with assets fixed in nominal terms, particularly those holding money and bonds and those with pensions that are not indexed to the cost of living. In the aggregate, it may be argued that this matter is a distributional question and only for private creditors and debtors, although the effects would be significant—gains for debtors and losses for creditors, the latter including many pensioners. But there would be substantial effects on the real value of the federal debt held by public. Currently at about $3.6 trillion, its real value to its holders would drop by $100 billion or more.[35] To those greatly (and improperly) worried about the federal debt, this real drop may seem fine. But to those directly or indirectly relying on their assets in the form of savings bonds and Treasury bills, notes, and bonds, it may be disquieting.

Of perhaps most consequence would be the changes in personal fortunes of losers at the lower end of the income distribution because of the rise in prices brought about by H-R-A. In the cases of some of the very poor with indexed government income support or assistance in kind, there would be some protection against the price inflation. But this protection would be incomplete. For millions of low-wage earners without government support the pain would be very great. These would be Americans whose incomes are already so low that they pay little in individual income taxes. They would hence gain little from the generous personal allowances or deductions totaling $34,700 for a family of four. The political discontent, to the extent that affected people vote, might prove much greater than that which brought the dramatic electoral changes of 1994.

A Better "Flat Tax"

I conclude by suggesting my ideal of sweeping tax reform that would correct all or almost all the faults in the current income tax system that the flat tax promises to eliminate, without most of its drawbacks. The Eisner program will certainly seem beyond the realm of political reality at this time. But then, despite the powerful support generated by Congressman Armey's name, I doubt that many, including Mr. Armey, would view his flat tax proposal as within the realm of current political reality. And I might add that some of my proposals could stand alone; all do not have to stand or fall together.

I would begin by eliminating the corporate income tax, lock, stock, and barrel. Let us recall the words of Hall and Rabushka: "Businesses do not pay taxes, individuals do." Let us then tax individuals directly so that we can get a reasonable idea of who is paying the taxes and how much. We would include all the earnings related to business activity—real interest, dividends, and real, accrued capital gains of owners—in individual income. Among the many advantages of eliminating the corporate income tax would be elimination of the double taxation of dividends, which biases the financial structure of corporations in the direction of internal financing and raising outside capital by debt rather than equity. Taxing real rather than nominal interest is an obviously desirable move that limits the tax to what is actually income and permits lenders to receive positive aftertax returns in periods of substantial inflation. Taxing real capital gains as they accrue, with full loss offset, would end the lock-in effect on holders of equity and hence improve the efficiency of capital markets. It would also make moot the step-up of basis at death. And of course it would eliminate the absurd and pernicious taxation of nominal capital gains that reflect only general inflation.[36]

I would also eliminate payroll taxes for social security. Putting their proceeds "in" trust funds is an accounting fiction. Our separate set of payroll taxes discriminates against labor income, which is also taxed in the individual income tax. And it does so, unlike the H-R-A "flat" wage tax, with no deductions and hence no progressivity. I would remove all taxes on social security benefits. Recipients will generally have paid taxes on their income, which we may still credit to their personal social security accounts. If social security income were to be taxed, I would gross it up so that the elderly suffer no general net loss as a consequence of the switch to a comprehensive tax.

I would also eliminate all other taxes, except estate and gift taxes, that cannot be justified as user taxes or taxes to attempt to equate individual and social cost. I would hence maintain—and increase—gasoline and cigarette taxes and, with a bit of hesitancy, maintain taxes on alcoholic beverages. (I refuse to believe that, taken in moderation, alcoholic beverages are bad.) I would, unlike Hall and Rabushka, retain estate and gift taxes as an instrument of our dedication to a free and fluid society, in which people are led to succeed by their own efforts and we try to moderate the influence of inherited wealth.[37]

I would then fold all other federal taxes into our new, comprehensive income tax. As with H-R-A, other than the standard personal deduction or allowance, all the myriad deductions, loopholes, and "tax expenditures" would be eliminated. In a number of cases, however, these would be replaced by up-front government spending. Among my recommended Treasury subsidies would be those for replacement (and expansion) of the earned-income tax credit; state and local taxes and taxable bonds (as a substitute for tax-exempt bonds); health care; owner-occupied housing; education and training; and basic research, all of which might come to no more than $200 billion, as compared with revenue losses from tax expenditures in the current tax code that amount to well over $500 billion.[38] I see important externalities in the activities that I would subsidize, particularly in the light of other aspects of the interface between government and the private sector.

But to realize these positive externalities, I would not reduce the measure of comprehensive income subject to taxation. I would even hope to add imputations for rental income produced in owner-occupied housing and some of the other corrections in the Bureau of Economic Analysis National Income and Product Accounts, such as the value of food and fuel consumed on farms; board, meals, and services furnished by employers to employees without charge or below cost; and services provided consumers by financial institutions in lieu of interest payments. The comprehensive base, with the inclusion of all real capital gains and interest on government securities, would indeed exceed national income.[39]

With the taxation of all capital income, including interest on state and local bonds, dividends, and real, accrued capital gains, as well as generous personal allowances as in H-R-A and the maintenance of an expanded earned-income credit, there might be sufficient progressivity even to permit the application of the cherished flat tax, albeit as in H-R-A, really at two rates, zero and some positive number. I would estimate, given my larger base, particularly with the inclusion of all capital income, that despite the elimination of payroll and other taxes, we could maintain revenue neutrality with the Armey personal deductions, which total $34,700 for a family of four, and a "flat" rate of 31.63 percent. This flat rate tax, it will be recalled, will replace current individual and corporate income taxes and payroll taxes. It is to be compared with a rate of 22.87 percent plus 13.85 percent in payroll taxes for social security and Medicare, or 36.72 percent, that the Armey bill would impose in direct taxes on labor income.[40] If we include only the smaller personal deductions of Hall and Rabushka, coming to $25,500 for a family of four, we would need a flat tax of only 27.10 percent, compared with the total of 32.85 percent in direct taxes that their proposal would place on labor income. The financing of the $200 billion of subsidies I have proposed would increase the flat tax rates to 37.63 percent with the Armey exemptions and 32.23 percent with the Hall and Rabushka exemptions. In either case, we would have a more progressive tax structure than what we have now.[41]

If it were desirable, however, to introduce more progressivity, I could readily accept and be induced to endorse a third tax rate, say 46 percent with the Armey exemptions, for really high incomes, say, over $350,000.[42] It might then be advisable to add an averaging feature for taxable income to avoid penalizing those whose incomes fluctuate from year to year across marginal rates. This complication would certainly be trivial as compared with H-R-A.[43] Except for that and trivially additional reporting necessary for fair and effective taxation of real capital gains, my comprehensive, more or less flat tax, then offers all the simplification advantages of H-R-A. It quite eliminates the monstrous system we have. But it does so in a way that is fair, almost flat, and not at all foolish.

Notes

1. Robert E. Hall and Alvin Rabushka, *Low Tax, Simple Tax, Flat Tax* (New York: McGraw-Hill, 1983); Hall and Rabushka, *The Flat Tax*, Second Edition (Stanford, Calif.: Hoover Institution Press, 1995); and chap. 2 of this volume.

2. Hall and Rabushka, *The Flat Tax*, p. 81, indicate that their proposal of a tax rate of 19 percent and allowances of $25,500 for families of four is equivalent to one with a tax rate of 23 percent and allowances of $34,500. Since they judge their proposal as revenue neutral in comparison with current law, they apparently judge the 23 percent–$34,500 parameters as also revenue neutral. But those are almost precisely the parameters of the Armey proposal—that would have allowances of $34,700 but might retain estate and gift taxes. Hall and Rabushka thus imply that the Armey version would require a 23 percent flat tax, not the 20 percent with which they would start, let alone the 17 percent rate that they propose for 1997 and beyond. My own estimates confirm the Hall and Rabushka evaluation, as

will be explained below. If their flat tax of 19 percent is in fact revenue neutral, I calculate, on the basis of projections from a sample of early returns for 1993, the year with which Hall and Rabushka were working, that it would take a 22.87 percent flat tax, with the parameters specified in the Armey bill, to bring in the same revenue as the current system.

3. As suggested by David Bradford in "What Are Consumption Taxes and Who Pays Them?" *Tax Notes*, April 18, 1988, pp. 383–91, and elsewhere in his "X-Tax," a consumption tax very much like H-R-A but with progressive rates on the wage tax.

4. See chapter 2 of this volume.

5. Hall and Rabushka, *The Flat Tax*, p.121.

6. Ibid., p. 124.

7. There can, of course, be other assumptions about the consequences of a general consumption tax, as pointed out in Joint Committee on Taxation, *Methodology and Issues in Measuring Changes in the Distribution of Tax Burden* (Washington, D.C.: U.S. Government Printing Office, 1993), which refers to a general increase in prices as "the traditional method of distributing a consumption tax" (p. 54). I find it appropriate in this instance to follow tradition.

The deductibility of wages in the business tax does add some complications, however. If there is a rising supply curve of labor in terms of the real wage, employers may be induced to raise nominal wages to avoid losing their workers. This would add to the upward push on prices, but, with wage deductibility prices would rise by less than the rise in pretax wage costs. If the supply curve is closer to vertical, as I would argue, if not backward bending, the reduction in labor supply would not occur and wages would not rise in response to the increase in prices. There would be some compensation for wage earners, particularly those with high incomes, in the form of lower personal taxes as compared with current law.

There are some further problems, which I shall ignore, with respect to forms of income such as social security benefits and in-kind medical benefits, which are indexed in whole or in part for inflation.

8. See David Bradford, *Untangling the Income Tax* (Cambridge, Mass.: Harvard University Press, 1986), p. 16; and Robert Eisner, *The Total Incomes System of Accounts* (Chicago: University

of Chicago Press, 1989), pp. 17–19.

9. See Robert Eisner, "The Permanent Income Hypothesis: Comment," *American Economic Review*, vol. 48, December 1958, pp. 972–90.

10. Since the aggregate increase in business taxes is exactly equal to the aggregate cut in individual taxes, households will in the aggregate have just enough of an increase in aftertax income to pay the increase in prices corresponding to the increase in business taxes.

11. Expanded income equals adjusted gross income plus tax-exempt interest plus workers' compensation plus nontaxable social security benefits plus excluded income of U.S. citizens living abroad plus value of Medicare benefits in excess of premiums paid plus minimum tax preferences plus employer contributions for health plans and life insurance plus employer share of payroll taxes plus corporate tax payments imputed to individual holders of corporate equity. The published estimates are to be found in Joint Committee on Taxation, *Methodology and Issues in Measuring Changes in the Distribution of Tax Burden* (Washington, D.C.: GPO, 1993), table 3, p. 55.

12. The lowest AGI classes undoubtedly include large amounts of negative transitory income, indeed even negative total incomes. Similarly, the higher AGI classes have average transitory incomes that are positive, contributing to the high measured income of these classes. Measures related to permanent income would probably show less regressivity. This reservation applies to all measures of progressivity regarding current income, to the flat tax as well as the current income tax.

Noting the paragraph above in an earlier draft, Hall declared in chapter 6 in this volume that, therefore, it "would be an improper inference from Eisner's calculations that the flat tax is less progressive than the income tax." His argument is somewhat disingenuous. Almost all public discussion of the burden of taxes is in terms of current, not permanent, income, however we may measure the latter. Proponents of the flat tax generally boast how much individual income taxes will be reduced as proportions of current, not permanent income.

Nothing, after all, is permanent. Taxpayers clearly must be concerned with their taxes in the here and now. And in any event, as indicated in the text above, neither appropriate measures of "permanent income" nor, a fortiori, averages of several years' income, can cause us to reject the inference that consumption is a sharply declining proportion of income. The poor consume all their income no matter how measured. And most of the middle class accumulates little wealth and consumes much of it over their lifetimes. Recent trends in the distribution of both income and wealth suggest that these relations are sharpening.

13. $6,350 for joint filers, $5,600 for "heads of households," $3,800 for singles, $3,175 for "married filing separately," and $2,450 for each dependent. By way of ready comparison, a family of four filing jointly would have exemptions of only $11,250 while the corresponding Hall and Rabushka personal allowances would be $26,500.

14. That is, over all AGI classes broken down in these tabulations. As we move to very high incomes, over $1,000,000, we may find regressivity developing to the extent larger and larger proportions of income are received in the form of lightly taxed capital gains. The inclusion of nontaxable interest would also decrease the progressivity or increase the regressivity as we move into upper-income groups.

15. In chapter 6 in this volume, Hall introduces as a measure of fairness a "proper version" of my table 3–13, relating the tax rate to consumption rather than income. I have indicated, above, my objections to excluding income and wealth and taking current "consumption"—and domestic consumption at that—as a sole measure of welfare. But the table proffered by Hall and Rabushka does not measure even the tax rate on consumption correctly. It considers the effect only of the individual wage tax, ignoring the repeated (correct) assertions by Hall and Rabushka that their business tax is a tax on consumption.

An appropriate comparison would begin with the figures, shown in my tables 3–11 to 3–13, indicating that while current business income taxes come to 5.95 percent of total income, the Hall and Rabushka version of the flat tax would bring that proportion to 9.07 percent and the Armey version to 10.91 percent. In terms of consumption, with personal consumption expenditures running about 80 percent of personal income, that means that the current business tax is at about 7.4 percent, the Hall and Rabushka tax rate is 11.3 percent, and the Armey rate comes to 13.6 percent. These last numbers apply to the flat taxes on consumption, due to the business tax, of those earning $10,000 and $20,000, as well as the taxes of all other consumption groups. They are well above the zero rates of Hall and Rabushka's "proper version" of my table and well above the total tax rates under current law, where families consuming only $10,000 or even $20,000 are not likely to have a great deal in the way of individual income tax liabilities. Wage earners, of course, under both current law and the flat tax also have substantial payroll taxes, with no deductions. By eliminating the earned-income tax credit, the flat tax would take away an offset to these taxes for low-wage workers and further increase the ratio of their taxes to their consumption.

16. The Armey-Shelby version of the flat tax (H.R. 2060 and S.1050, "The Freedom and Fairness Restoration Act"), introduced July 19, 1995, would reduce the standard deduction for a family of four to $31,400. The Treasury estimates that it would require a rate of 20.8 percent for revenue neutrality, which squares roughly with the rate of 22.87 percent that I calculated for the original Armey proposal with the higher deductions. The Armey-Shelby proposal, with revenue neutrality, would be fairly similar to the original Armey plan in its distribution of taxes but somewhat more regressive for those above low income levels.

The flat tax proposed by Steve Forbes when he was a presidential candidate would have lowered taxes in all income brackets. This would have been accomplished with a tax rate of 17 percent, exemptions for a family of four that came to $36,000, and no tax on pensions. With these parameters, however, there would have been a net loss of tax revenues of some $200 billion. For revenue neutrality it would clearly have required a rate well above the 22.87 percent of the original Armey proposal and, a fortiori, above Armey-Shelby and Hall and Rabushka.

17. *Budget of the United States Government, Analytical Perspectives, Fiscal Year 1995* (Washington, D.C.: GPO, 1994), Table 6.6, p. 77.

18. See Robert Eisner, "Capital Gains and Income: Real Changes in the Value of Capital in the United States, 1945–1975," in Dan Usher, ed., *The Measurement of Capital* (Chicago: Univer-

sity of Chicago Press for National Bureau of Economic Research, 1980), pp. 175–342; and Eisner, *The Total Incomes System of Accounts* (Chicago: University of Chicago Press, 1989).

19. Hall and Rabushka, *The Flat Tax*, p. 100.

20. Capital gains along with other capital income already largely escape taxation in pension funds. The complete elimination of capital income taxation at the individual level, along with the consequent increase in liquidity of individually held assets, may be expected to generate a shift of investment from pension funds to direct individual investments.

21. $(1.0907/1.0595) - 1 = 0.0294479$; $(1.1091/1.0595) - 1 = 0.0468145$.

22. These figures are merely rough illustrations. They assume that tax depreciation is taken only at each anniversary of capital acquisition and that accelerated depreciation, which would reduce the differential if applied to both investments, is not used.

23. See, for example, Hall and Rabushka, *The Flat Tax*, pp. 87, 127, and chapter 2 in this volume.

24. Chapter 6 in this volume.

25. Hall and Rabushka, *The Flat Tax*, p. 110.

26. It is not clear that H-R-A would deduct business expenses even on training for management and workers in calculating the business tax. Would an executive education program at Northwestern University, or elsewhere, bc counted as a deductible business expense, compensation of employees, or a form of fringe benefit?

27. Eisner, "Extended Measures of National Income and Product" and *The Total Incomes System of Accounts.*

28. Robert Haveman and Barbara Wolfe, "The Determinants of Children's Attainments: A Review of Methods and Findings," *Journal of Economic Literature*, vol. 33, no. 4 (December 1995), p. 1830.

29. Chapter 6 in this volume.

30. The marginal tax on labor may indeed be taken in Hall and Rabushka to be $19 + 6.2 + 1.45 + (1.19 * 6.2) = 34.028$ percent. Applying the Armey rate apparently necessary for revenue neutrality we have $22.87 + 6.2 + 1.45 + (1.2287 * 6.2) = 38.138$ percent. (These figures do not include the federal unemployment insurance tax [FUTA], which is 6.2 percent minus a 5.4 percent credit for state taxes but has a low federal cap, at $7,000.)

31. The large increases in labor, resulting in a 6 percent increase in output, which they predicted on the basis of their interpretation of work by Jerry Hausman, was early challenged by Joseph Pechman in his review of the first edition of Hall and Rabushka, *Low Tax, Simple Tax, Flat Tax*. See Joseph Pechman, Review of Hall and Rabushka, *Low Tax, Simple Tax, Flat Tax, Journal of Political Economy* (1985), pp. 340–43.

32. As indicated by Hall and Rabushka, *The Flat Tax*, p. 63, and chapter 1 in this volume.

33. *Budget of the United States Government, Analytical Perspectives*, Fiscal Year 1996, p. 41.

34. Hall and Rabushka, *The Flat Tax*, pp. 65-66.

35. The Hall-Rabushka business tax might be expected, as pointed out above, to raise prices by $(1.0907/1.0595) - 1$, or 2.945 percent; the loss in purchasing power of the dollar is $1 - 1/1.02945 = 2.86$ percent. Multiplying this number by \$3.6 trillion for the debt gives a figure of \$103 billion. Similar calculations for the Armey business tax, with its 10.91 percent effective rate, indicate an exogenous upward push to prices of 4.681 percent and a loss in the purchasing power of the dollar of 4.47 percent, amounting to a \$160.9 billion reduction in the real value of the existing federal debt.

36. Taxation of real, accrued capital gains can be easily accomplished for owners of listed securities. We could merely have corporations report to their stockholders (and to the IRS) the averages of the highs and lows for stock prices on the last trading day of each year. The IRS for its part would make known the inflation percentage to apply to the initial prices of securities held for the entire year. More detail, in terms of adjustments by month for securities acquired during the year, could readily be added. Computing accrued capital gains for assets for which transaction prices were not established could be accomplished by relying on taxpayer declaration of values at the end of each year. To the extent he misestimates them, he would compensate—with appropriate interest or other penalties—at realization or death. This procedure would apply as well to owners of unincorporated business, who would be taxed only on what they take out of their business and their real, accrued capital gains. There would be no business tax returns of any kind, no elaborate depreciation calculations—nothing! Individuals would be

permitted to deduct their out-of-pocket expenses incurred in connection with earning their income.

37. Armey's H.R. 4585 makes no mention of estate and gift taxes, which implies that they would be retained. This inclusion is put in some doubt, however, by his avowal that his bill is essentially an implementation of the flat tax proposal of Hall and Rabushka, who call explicitly for their abandonment.

38. See *Budget of the United States, Analytical Perspectives,* Fiscal Year 1996, table 5.1, pp. 40–42, which lists total revenue losses for tax expenditures in the income tax but does not total them, presumably because of interaction of the revenue effects of the various tax expenditures.

39. An indication of just how much a truly comprehensive income tax base would exceed the base in current law may be gleaned from Susan C. Nelson, "Family Economic Income and Other Income Concepts Used in Analyzing Tax Reform," in Office of Tax Analysis, Department of the Treasury, *Compendium of Tax Research* 1987 (Washington, D.C.: GPO, 1987). She derives a measure of "family economic income" that exceeds 1983 AGI (based on the pre-1986 tax law) by almost 50 percent and somewhat exceeds personal income for that year as well. Hall and Rabushka arrive at a total of $5,003 billion for the 1993 bases of their business tax and wage tax before allowances. This total, without capital income, comes close to the 1993 figures of $5,131 billion for national income and $5,375 billion for personal income.

40. As observed above, we should add to this the 22.87 percent business tax on the 6.2 percent employer contributions for social security, or 1.42 percent, which would bring the total to 38.14 percent.

41. I estimate these figures, roughly, by assuming that I could build the comprehensive base to about $5,600 billion (calculating in terms of 1993 figures). The exemptions under the Armey plan come, by my estimates reported above, to $2,263.173 billion, and with Hall and Rabushka to $1,705 billion. Total income and payroll taxes to be replaced amount to $1,055.5 billion. I would add $200 billion of direct expenditures. We thus have $1,255.5 billion to be raised on a base of $3,336.827 billion with the Armey exemptions, which implies a 37.626 percent flat rate. With the Hall and Rabushka exemptions the

taxable base is raised to \$3,895 billion. The necessary tax rate is thus reduced to 32.23 percent. Without the additional direct expenditures, the taxes to be raised are reduced to \$1,055.5 and the flat tax rates to 31.632 percent and 27.099 percent.

42. In chapter 6 in this volume, Hall finds "startling" "my easy concession" that I could accept a marginal rate as high as 46 percent in a unitary income plan for really high incomes such as those over \$350,000. I wish he would express more shock and dismay at effective rates of over 100 percent for those considering a job that might take them off welfare. But it must be emphasized that my 46 percent would entail the elimination of all other income-related taxes, including the 13.85 percent in payroll taxes for social security and Medicare. It is not that much higher than the 36.72 percent total in a revenue-neutral Armey flat tax for all wage earners with incomes over \$34,700. And it is significantly below the current-law figures of 39.6 percent plus 13.85 percent, for a total of 53.45 percent that begins, for joint filers, at \$77,262 of taxable income.

43. The flat tax on wages would actually have, as we have pointed out, two rates: the rate of 19 percent (or 20 percent or 22.87 percent) and zero. There is hence a need to avoid penalties for those who are at the zero rate one year, not using up their personal deductions, but then paying taxes at the positive flat rate the next. Neither Hall and Rabushka nor Armey provides for negative taxes or refunds so that taxpayers with incomes that fluctuate above and below the zero rate point are penalized.

4

Why America Needs the Flat Tax

Dick Armey

W hy do we need the Hall and Rabushka flat tax? Our current tax code is a wasteful, complicated mess. It is so bad that even the Internal Revenue Service cannot always give accurate advice on it. Today, the average family pays more in taxes than it spends on food, clothing, and shelter combined. Nearly 40 percent of the nation's income is now spent, not by the workers who earned it, but by the government that taxed it from them. Of all the supposed crises we are facing today, this is one of the most serious.

How the Tax Works

My plan launches an assault on big government on three fronts—taxes, spending, and regulation. But the centerpiece of the plan is the tax system, based on the Hall-Rabushka flat tax first proposed in 1985. Rather than tinkering, we would scrap the entire tax code and start over. It would work like this. All income would be taxed once and only once at the single low rate of 17 percent, and there would be a generous family allowance to go with the tax on wages. And that is it. We would eliminate the whole existing tangle of deductions and credits. Instead,

This chapter was originally presented as a talk at an American Enterprise Institute conference on the flat tax on January 27, 1995. It has been edited for publication.

in 1997 there would be a family allowance of $13,100 for an individual, $26,200 for a married couple, and $5,300 for each child. A family of four would have to earn $36,800 before it owed a penny of federal income tax. And then that family would pay only 17 percent on everything above that amount. Business income would be handled with equal simplicity. A corporation would simply subtract expenses from revenues and pay a 17 percent rate on the remainder. That is it. This is as simple as an income tax gets.

We phase in the 17 percent rate. We decided to set the rate at 20 percent in the first and second years and then lower it to 17 percent in the third year. A 20 percent rate will lose perhaps $40 billion on a conventional static estimate, but we make up that loss in spending cuts listed in the bill. These spending cuts, together with greater economic growth unleashed by the flat tax, will enable us to afford the lower 17 percent rate in year three. We want to plow the revenue windfall into a lower tax rate, not more government.

What will happen? No longer will Americans spend anything like 5.4 billion man-hours figuring their taxes each year. No longer will the IRS have to send out 8 billion pages of paper every year. No longer will the special interests be able to work their political mischief. Nor will the social engineers be able to conduct their experiments in the tax code. And, of course, legions of lawyers and accountants will need to find other work. But my favorite part is that we will be able to pay our taxes on a form the size of a postcard.

A Growth Bonanza

The flat tax will spark an economic growth bonanza. Any economist will tell you that the surest way for a family to increase its wages is through greater work, savings, and investment. The flat tax expands all three. By lowering the top marginal income tax rate from 40 percent to 17 percent, it encourages work. By ending the current double taxation of savings—sweeping away the estate tax, the capital gains tax, and the tax on interest and dividends—it creates a tremendous new incentive to save. And by permitting businesses to deduct all wages and purchases of plant and equipment immediately, it replaces today's complicated maze of depreciation schedules, credits, and other politically targeted tax breaks with a simple, neutral system that will spur a boom in capital investment.

One of the causes of today's middle-class anxiety is slow wage growth. Over the past twenty-five years, real wages have grown at about half the rate of the preceding twenty-five years. Increased investment will raise the productivity of our workers and revive wages. And that requires capital: the equipment, the tools, and the computers that workers use to expand output. Capital is the lifeblood of an economy and a key to higher wages and living standards. Unfortunately, today's double taxation of savings dampens investment and shrinks the pool of capital available to entrepreneurs.

On this issue, all the major tax reform plans before Congress agree. Whether it is the Nunn-Domenici USA consumption tax, the national sales tax, the value-added tax, or the flat tax, all these plans agree that we need to end the discriminatory treatment of savings. But none of these proposals can match the simplicity, the low marginal rates, and the visibility of the flat tax. To put it bluntly, the flat tax will do more to help every American get rich than is possible with today's code or any of the alternative proposals.

From an economic standpoint, the flat tax is ideal because it is perfectly neutral. It maintains neutrality between types and sizes of business, between economic sectors, and between types of investment. Its motto might be "All power to the people!" because it transfers all decision-making power from the hands of planners to the hands of private citizens.

Tax Withholding

My plan goes beyond the Hall and Rabushka proposal in this respect. It takes aim at the crucial, deceptive device that has made big government possible—income tax withholding. If America had not accepted withholding as a "temporary" wartime measure in 1943 and if taxpayers had continued paying their taxes the same way they have always made rent or car payments, the government could never have grown as large as it has. Only by taking people's money before they ever see it has the government been able to raise taxes to their current height without sparking a revolt.

This point was brought home for me when I had the pleasure of spending the weekend with my son, David. He was rejoicing that the government was sending him some money in a refund check. And I thought, "Lord have mercy, he's a smart boy, he's a good boy. Where did I go wrong?" And I told him, "Why don't you go back and look at one of your pay stubs and multiply by twelve? Then see if you're so happy that the government is giving you a pittance of your own money back." At our next conversation, his rejoicing had turned into a healthy anger. And he said something that reminded me of what my mother used to say, "What are all those dang fools doin' with my money!"

By ending withholding, we put a permanent check on the confiscatory appetites of the political class. You may ask, "Will people still pay their taxes?" I am confident they would. I think if the American people have a tax system that is honest, direct, simple, low, and fair, they will comply. In fact, I believe my plan will actually lead to less cheating and a smaller underground economy.

A Fair Tax

Already, the Beltway liberals are calling the flat tax "unfair," a code word for not progressive. But the fact of the matter is that the generous family allowances will have a progressive effect, for two reasons. First, they take millions of poor people right off the rolls. And second, the family allowances are worth more, the less you make. Let me give you some examples. A family of four making $36,000 would pay zero percent of its income. A family making $50,000 would pay 4.5 percent of its income. And a family making $200,000 would pay 14 percent of its income. That is progressive. And if experience is any guide, the rich will end up paying more taxes when the rates come down, which is exactly what happened after the Coolidge tax cuts of the 1920s, the Kennedy tax cuts of 1964, and the Reagan cuts of 1981.

Fairness is, in fact, one of the great virtues of the flat tax. It treats everyone the same. Rather than have fallible politicians decide, for their own reasons, which groups should render more or less of their earnings to the government, the flat tax sets a single objective standard: no matter how much money a person makes, no matter what kind of business he is in, and no matter where he invests his savings, he will be taxed at the same rate as everyone else.

The flat tax would raise revenue efficiently. It would unleash the economic talents and energies of American workers and businesses. And it would allow all Americans, including the risk takers and the job creators, to enjoy the fruits of their labor in freedom.

We flat taxers are populists. We flat-taxers think the vast resources of this great commercial nation can be better allocated over kitchen tables than over Capitol Hill's green felt tables. We believe government should be open, honest, direct—and smaller. And most Americans agree with us. I hope to see my plan ride a populist prairie fire of enthusiasm to final enactment in the 104th Congress. But if that proves too ambitious a timetable, then I hope to see the flat tax endorsed in the 1996 Republican platform and signed into law under the next Republican president—in 1997.

Like a powerful locomotive gathering speed, the flat

tax is an idea that cannot be stopped. It has already sparked a healthy national debate about the current system. Doubtless as that debate gathers momentum, we will see the special interests running alongside the train, demanding that we slam on the brakes. We will see the class-warriors try to slow us down with false claims about progressivity. We will see the fans of big government laying down on the tracks, trying to scare us with their claims about widows, orphans, and the end of civilization as we know it. But in the end, I believe the American people will disregard the special interests and choose the national interest. Carried forward by the flat tax, we will reach our destination of freedom, fairness, and prosperity for all.

5

The Uneasy Case for the Flat Tax

Herbert Stein

About forty years ago, when all right-thinking people believed that the progressive income tax was the ideal form of tax, two University of Chicago professors, Harry Kalven and Walter Blum, wrote an incisive article called, "The Uneasy Case for Progressive Taxation." The article did not show that the progressive income tax was a bad tax. It showed only that many of the things said for it were unproved and probably unprovable.

What Kalven and Blum said about the progressive income tax could probably be said about any specific tax. Now with the rush to embrace the flat tax, it is time to remind ourselves that the case for it too is uneasy.

Changes in the System

Introduction of the flat tax would change the present system of income taxation in two ways: first, it would change the base of the tax; second, it would flatten the rate. These are two quite different things.

Presumably changing the base will increase its size. Expanding the base would permit a "reduction" of the rate within a revenue-neutral policy. Actually, what happens is a reduction of the rate on what was previously included in the base and an increase in the rate on what was not previously included. Thus, the inclusion of employer-provided health benefits in taxable income would permit a reduction of the rate on wage income paid in cash but entails an increase of the rate on wage income paid in health benefits. Not all the base changes involved in moving to the flat tax, however, would be base broadening. At least one would reduce the base: the deduction of gross investment rather than depreciation from taxable income. I will return to the question of the base later.

But even if the expansion of the base permits a reduction of the effective rate on the base, and if that is considered a gain, that is not an argument for a flat rate. Although it might be clear that a rate schedule running from 10 to 30 percent is better than one running from 15 to 35 percent, it does not follow that a flat rate of 20 percent is better than one running from 10 to 30. The fairness question does not permit of an objective answer, and the economic consequences are ambiguous.

Argument for the Flat Tax

Much of the argument for the flat tax is that it will greatly simplify the preparation of tax returns. But that simplification results almost entirely from the redefinition of the base and hardly at all from the flatness of the tax. If taxable income is calculated in the manner that permits it to be reported entirely on a postcard, applying a graduated tax rate to that income will not be a complicated matter. Anyone could read his or her tax liability from a tax schedule.

What seems to be the main practical reason for the proposed flatness of the tax is that it simplifies the integration of the corporate tax and the individual tax. In the flat tax, all capital income earned in corporations is taxed at the corporate level only and at the same rate as all labor income is taxed at the individual level. Then all income is presumably taxed at the same rate. If different individuals paid different rates on their wage income, there would be no way to apply the same rate to their corporate capital income without allocating all the capital income to its individual beneficiaries, a procedure difficult in the case of undistributed corporate profits.

But the flat tax does not really solve this problem. The flat-tax proposal involves a personal exemption from income tax for labor income up to a specified level. Suppose, for ease of calculation, that the exemption level for a family of four is $30,000 and the flat tax rate is 20 percent. Then a family with $60,000 of labor income would pay a tax of $6,000, and a family with $60,000 of capital income from investments would pay a tax of $12,000. Such a rate does not seem very "flat," and its fairness may not appeal to everyone. One may say that the marginal tax rate is the same for both, but we usually do not think of fairness in terms of marginal rates.

In fact, the marginal rates are not flat either. In the example given, a flat marginal rate of 20 percent of the excess of labor income over $30,000 applies *if the excess is positive.* But if the excess is negative, the marginal rate is zero. Thus, a family with a labor income of $25,000 pays no more tax than a family with a labor income of $15,000. The family with a capital income of $25,000 pays $2,000 more tax than one with a capital income of $15,000.

Within the logic of the flat tax, the reason for the two-rate system—a positive rate on the excess of wage income over the exemption if the excess is positive and a zero rate if the excess is negative—is hard to understand. Presumably, the reason for levying no tax on a family with labor income of $30,000 (in my example) is that a tax of more than zero would be unfair—too much of a burden. If that is the case, a tax of zero on a family with labor income of $15,000 would be an even more excessive burden. Fairness would seem to require that the 20 percent rate be applied to the excess of the income over the exemption whether the excess was positive or negative. If the family had labor income of $15,000, its negative excess would be $15,000, and it would get a refund of $3,000. This system would also keep the marginal tax on labor income and on capital income equal at all income levels.

The Tax Base

Regarding the question of the tax base, proponents of the flat tax sometimes say (and sometimes admit) that it is really a tax on consumption. This is demonstrated in the following way. Suppose that all income is earned in the production of consumer goods and the production of investment goods. If we allow the deduction from income of all expenditures for the purchase of investment goods, what is left in the tax base is expenditure for the purchase of consumption goods. Net saving takes the form of the excess of gross capital investment over depreciation. That amount is now included in taxable income and would be excluded under the flat tax.

Whether consumption is a fairer tax base than income is another question to which there is no possible objective answer. (I postpone for the moment the question whether the flat tax in a consumption tax or not.) Suppose two people each spend $80,000 on consumption in a year; one has a wage income of $100,000 above any personal exemption, and the other has a wage income of $1,000,000 above any personal exemption. Is it fair, or "equal treatment" as proponents of the flat tax like to say, that they each should pay the same amount of tax? Would anyone but an economist, or the person with the $1,000,000 income, say so? One might say that the person with the $1,000,000 income is only deferring the payment of tax and that at infinity, when everyone has cashed in his chips, the amount of tax paid by each will be equal. But that seems a long time to wait.

Taxing income rather than consumption probably discourages the postponement of consumption—which is to say that it discourages saving. But not taxing saved income requires taxing something else more, and that also discourages some kind of economic behavior. It can dis-

105

courage work in favor of leisure. It can encourage consumption in less-taxed forms like the use of an owner-occupied home. Excluding the excess of gross investment over depreciation from the tax base distorts decisions in favor of long-lived assets. Excluding from the tax base investment in physical capital but not in human capital, as in education, also distorts economic decisions. We know very little about the magnitude of any of these effects, and so we know very little about the contribution that would be made to economic efficiency or growth by the shift to a flat tax of the kind now being proposed. That is to say, if the shift from an income tax to a consumption tax is not considered fair, one cannot be sure that there are sufficient efficiency and growth gains to outweigh that objection.

But even if one wants a consumption tax, the flat-tax route is a peculiar way to get there. It is not true that consumption is equal to income earned in domestic production minus gross private investment. Consumption equals income earned in domestic production minus gross private investment minus net exports minus government purchases of goods and services. Or the base of the flat tax, which is income earned in domestic production minus gross private investment, equals consumption plus net exports plus government purchases. Why net exports should be included in the base of a consumption tax is a mystery. It is also unclear whether government purchases should be considered consumption and, if so, whose consumption it is.

Moreover, the preceding calculations apply to the aggregate national tax base. When we come to the base of the tax of the individual taxpayer, which is what counts, there is a further qualification. An individual's saving includes the purchase of assets from other individuals, but the individual gets no tax relief for that. Thus if A and B have equal labor incomes, they will pay equal taxes; but if A sells assets to B, he can consume more than B. Or if A sells assets in the national market, reducing his portfolio, he can increase his consumption without increasing his tax, and whoever buys the assets will be reducing his consumption but will get no tax credit for it.

Elusive Interpretation

The flat tax has a "now you see it, now you don't" quality that makes its interpretation very elusive. In one light, it is a tax on income, with a deduction for saving. But, as noted, the deduction seems only partial. Moreover, the deduction is indirect and barely visible. The deduction is effected by grossing up the value of saving invested in business capital. Thus, omitting the personal exemption just for the sake of simplicity, we may take the case of a taxpayer with $100,000 of income. He pays a tax of $20,000, spends $20,000 on consumption, and invests $60,000 in the newly issued stock of a corporation. This purchase permits the corporation to buy $75,000 of capital equipment, because the deduction of that much investment from its income will save it $15,000 of taxes. So the individual taxpayer ends up with $75,000 of assets and $20,000 of consumption. He has paid only $5,000 of net taxes, which is 20 percent of his income minus his saving, because $15,000 of the gross tax of $20,000 has been offset by the corporation's tax saving on his behalf.

Alternatively, the flat tax can be regarded as a sales tax on consumption, or on the value of consumption goods produced in the domestic private sector. This view implies that with the imposition of the flat tax, all before-tax incomes earned in the private sector will rise by the amount of the tax, so that the imposition of the tax leaves aftertax income unchanged (and incomes below the exemption level increased). Then the prices of consumer goods rise by the amount of the tax, reducing the real income of individuals in proportion to their consumption.

Viewed in this way, the whole purpose of the tax at the individual level, which can be paid with a postcard, is

107

to establish qualification for exemption from the sales tax. A somewhat similar result, even better, could be performed with a sales tax and a flat per capita refund for every resident. John Doe would not have to report his income, only his existence. The required postcard return could be very simple, like this:

> Dear IRS:
> My name is John Doe, social security number 123-45-6789. I have a lovely wife and two fine children. Please send me $6,000.
> Having wonderful time, wish you were here.

Whether the markets would work to make these two processes, the sales tax and the income tax, come out the same way is not clear. But the two different possible pictures probably contribute to the salability of the plan—one picture being appealing to those to whom income tax is a bad name and one to those to whom sales tax is a bad name. That is another way of saying that it is difficult for the citizen to tell on what and on whom the tax really falls.

Alternatives to the Flat Tax

From almost any standpoint, the present federal income tax is full of anomalies, distortions, and complexity. This is a good time to think seriously about how to correct it. While the flat tax would correct the present system by eliminating it, there are other ways to correct it. Basically, there are three questions:

- Do we want an income tax or a consumption tax?
- How graduated should the rates of either be?
- How comprehensive should either be?

The flat tax is a consumption tax with slight graduation of rates. The Nunn-Domenici proposal, now in Congress, calls for a consumption tax with rates more graduated than the flat tax.

The existing income tax could be made more comprehensive and less distortive by covering kinds of income now excluded, such as fringe benefits and the imputed rent of owner-occupied homes. Those changes would permit lowering of rates, and the rates could be either more or less graduated than at present. Another possibility would be to eliminate or reduce substantially the taxation of corporate profits.

A radical version of the foregoing would be the Henry Simons–style of income tax, eliminating the corporate tax entirely and taxing comprehensively all personal income, including capital gains, at the same rate as other income. The rate of the income tax could be flat, on income above a personal exemption, as proposed by Milton Friedman in 1962, or graduated.

A still more radical reform would be to combine two Friedman proposals—a flat positive tax rate on personal income, comprehensively defined, on income above the exemption level, and a flat negative rate on income below the exemption level. This plan would have the incidental advantage of straightening out the taxation of capital gains by providing a refund for net capital losses in excess of ordinary income.

There is plenty of room for tax reform. Proponents of reform have no reason to allow flat taxers to monopolize the stage.

6

Response to Armey, Eisner, and Stein

Robert E. Hall

Congressman Dick Armey's support for the flat tax is encouraging and gratifying to its academic proponents. I concur in his belief that simplification is a central benefit of the flat tax. Not only does simplification yield direct benefits in reducing the resources wasted by the tax system, but also simplification seems to be the core of the flat tax's political appeal. We need to adopt a consumption tax to improve incentives to save and the flat tax is the best way to tax consumption. Many of the reasons for the latter conclusion appear in my response to Herbert Stein's skeptical remarks on this topic. I also concur in Armey's vigorous insistence that the flat tax is fair and progressive, thanks to its high family exemption.

Armey proposes to eliminate withholding. I can see the benefit of this change—today far too many people view the income tax as a benefit program because they receive tax refund checks. Withholding, though, is the key to the remarkably high compliance rate that the tax system achieves for wage and salary income.

Stein's Views

Herbert Stein, a good friend of tax reform, raises many specific criticisms of the flat tax. Without formulating a specific alternative, he advises against what he fears is an impending monopolization of the reform movement by the flat tax. It is my hope that the appeal of the flat tax is that it solves the tax reform problem better than the alternatives do. I think there are good answers to all Stein's criticisms—I will touch on some of the more important ones.

Income Tax versus Consumption Tax. Stein concludes that no objective answer resolves the question of choice between income and consumption as the base for taxation. I disagree. A fundamental proposition of modern public finance theory holds that intermediate products should not be taxed—taxation should be limited to products delivered to final users. In an economy operating over time, capital is an intermediate product. A related proposition is that if we restate an income tax as a consumption tax on current and future consumption, the tax rate on future consumption rises toward infinity with time. Zero taxation of the earnings of capital gives the desirable pattern of equal tax rates on consumption at all times. And if there is any other distortion for capital good, like some monopoly power in the capital goods industries, we might want to go beyond a consumption tax and put some subsidy on capital. The case for a consumption tax over an income tax is solid, with no issue of fairness in the choice—any income tax system can be replaced by a consumption tax that makes everyone better off.

Contrary to Stein's statement, a consumption tax does not distort the choice of investment toward longer-lived capital goods. Rather, an income tax distorts choices toward short-lived capital goods. An income tax raises the required rate of return, which is a larger factor in the investment decision for long-lived capital. A consumption tax does not distort the required rate of return. A consumption tax is neutral with respect to that and many other dimensions of choice. Similarly, there need be no distor-

111

tion favoring owner-occupied housing. The Hall and Rabushka proposal, with first-year write-off for landlords and the imposition of the tax on the production of new houses, gives exact neutrality between the two forms of housing. I will elaborate on this point in dealing with Robert Eisner's commentary.

Net Exports. Surprisingly, Stein allies himself with those who think that the rebate of tax for exports and imposition of tax on imports is beneficial. Although this opinion is common among politicians, I know of no other economist who shares it. The standard view among economists is that it is a matter of indifference to include or exclude net exports in a consumption tax, because the present discounted value of net exports is close to zero. And the exclusion of net exports makes for a much easier transition to the flat tax. If exports are excluded and imports included in the tax base, the dollar must appreciate by the amount of the tax at the time the tax is introduced. The alternative of including net exports causes no shock in the foreign exchange market. For that reason, the case is strong for following the Hall and Rabushka proposal; Stein's alternative would cause completely unnecessary and large windfalls in the foreign exchange market.

Lack of Exemption for Business Income. Stein is correct that the unusual family with income from capital but no wages or pensions would not benefit from the exemption in the flat tax. The actual number of such families is vanishingly small. For people directly involved in operating businesses, the problem does not arise because they would be allowed to pay themselves salaries so as to benefit from the exemption.

Family Exemptions. The only reason for the individual tax is to handle the exemption—why not just write families checks for their exemptions? Stein is quite right that the main reason for having an individual tax is to support family exemptions. We could roll the flat tax's business and individual taxes into a single tax, and it would just be a value-added tax but would not have an exemption. The problem is to find a good way to provide the exemption. Stein's idea that people would just tell the government about their existence and get a check for the value of their exemptions is naive. Policing false claims for exemptions would be a multibillion dollar headache for the IRS, as it is today under the earned-income tax credit. Would people who are in the United States for only four months out of a year get a third of the standard exemption? How can we verify the time they were here? The only workable answer is to key the exemption amount to earnings in the United States. I also think Armey has an important point that the government should not write checks unless it has to. If the only visible part of the tax system is a rebate check for $6,000, many people will have a completely false idea of what the government is taking from them. I find the reasons for setting up the exemption as part of a personal tax compelling—the choice is hardly the arbitrary one that Stein suggests.

Another important benefit of the individual part of the tax arises during the transition. Under the current tax system, workers are paid on a before-tax basis. After their wages are determined, they actually receive the agreed-upon amount less withholding. If we switched to a sales tax, as Stein proposes, or to a value-added tax, workers would expect to continue to be paid the agreed-upon amount, but they would no longer have to pay taxes. Their employers would have to pay the tax instead. Prices would have to rise enough to cover the increased tax cost. Thus, the switch to a sales or value-added tax would have to bring a one-time wave of inflation, worse than anything seen previously in U.S. history. This inflation would occur because the full amount of tax payments would be distributed as an increase in the prices of goods and services. With the flat tax, no inflation at all would arise from the wage tax part of our proposal. Workers would continue to be paid on a pretax basis and would continue to pay tax out of their earnings. The practical significance of this difference is overwhelming but is not mentioned in Stein's claim that a sales tax would be just as convenient as the flat tax.

Not a Measure of Consumption. The flat tax claims to be a consumption tax but does not actually measure a family's consumption. The claim is correct. It is not necessary to keep track of each family's whole budget to tax its consumption. After all, a sales tax on all consumption goods is certainly a consumption tax but does not measure anything at the family level. A value-added tax is equivalent to a sales tax but is much easier to administer. The flat tax is just a value-added tax with part of the tax paid by workers. Its economic effect is the same as a sales tax. Stein is right that someone looking at the tax forms will not see at a glance that it is a consumption tax. But the flat tax does create an environment in which saving earns a greater reward than it does under an income tax. What people cannot tell from the tax returns they can tell from the signals they get from the market.

Alternatives. Stein concludes agnostically that we ought to be thinking about the Nunn-Domenici personal consumption tax or an income tax with a broader base as meritorious alternatives to the flat tax. The personal consumption tax, which keeps track of every element of a family's budget, utterly fails to deliver the benefits of simplification, a benefit that Armey properly stresses. The Nunn-Domenici tax, as currently proposed, is a frightening step backward in terms of near-confiscatory taxation of successful people and businesses, because the top rate on taxable income over $24,000 would be 40 percent. The proposal would tax higher-income taxpayers at a 40 percent rate and would impose an 11 percent value-added tax as well, for a combined rate of 51 percent. Income taxes miss the essential benefit of lifting taxation from a key intermediate product, capital. A consumption tax can always beat an income tax. At a minimum, I would urge Stein to limit the range of his agnosticism to alternative consumption taxes.

Eisner's Views

Robert Eisner pushes even harder against the flat tax. He is a fan of base broadening and welcomes the integration of corporate and personal taxation to eliminate the double taxation of dividends. But he is adamant in his opposition to consumption taxation.

Critique of Consumption Taxation. Eisner clearly favors income over consumption taxation, although he does not spend much space making the argument. As I noted in my response to Stein, modern public finance theory has created a strong presumption in favor of consumption taxation. Income taxation—by taxing an intermediate product—puts a completely avoidable inefficiency into the economy, one that everyone has to pay for. It is just as inefficient to tax the earnings of capital as it would be to put a special tax on industrial use of steel.

Eisner does offer one argument that survives this point. He observes that if the effect of military spending is to protect physical capital, then the earnings of capital should be taxed at a rate that reflects the additional military spending made necessary by another unit of capital. Not since the War of 1812 has an enemy damaged U.S. capital, and the risk today seems negligible. The general principle Eisner enunciates, that capital should bear its fair share of the cost of government, is dead wrong in the thinking of modern public finance.

Distribution of the Burden of the Flat Tax. Eisner presents some extensive calculations of the amount of tax paid by

115

income category. His calculations in table 3–16 seem to suggest that the existing tax system is regressive and the flat tax would be even more regressive. His note 12 shows admirable candor in revealing why these calculations should be disregarded; I would put much more weight on the note than Eisner does. Some of the families in low AGI categories are poor, but others are not. They are able to continue consuming—and therefore paying a consumption tax—because their low AGIs are purely transitory. Eisner's estimate in table 3–13 that families in the lowest income category would pay a flat tax equal to an astonishing 31 percent of their incomes shows how useless these calculations are. Eisner does not mention that low-income families (the 20 percent with the lowest incomes) pay 80 percent of their incomes for housing, 30 percent for transportation, 38 percent for food, and 48 percent for "other" goods and services. (See "Indicators," *The American Enterprise,* vol. 6, no. 1 [January/February 1995], p. 17.) Their total consumption is several times their incomes.

It is an axiom of economists' thinking—reflected in Eisner's note 12—that income in a single year, such as AGI, is a highly misleading way to look at distributional issues. We need either a measure of permanent income or a measure of consumption to get any kind of picture of the distribution of tax burdens. It is essential that the low categories be restricted to the genuinely poor and that the high categories be genuinely rich. The confusion that results from defying the principle of note 12 is not random; it is the systematic conclusion that the tax system is much more regressive than it really is. The artificial bias toward regressiveness is greater for a consumption tax than for an income tax. To infer from Eisner's calculations that the flat tax is less progressive than the income tax would be improper.

Because the flat tax is a strict consumption tax, there is little mystery about the distribution of its burden across consumption groups. Wages below the exemption level of

$25,500 for a family of four are untaxed. Wages above that level are taxed at 19 percent. The proper version of Eisner's table 3–13, as I look at the issue, is:

Consumption (thousands of dollars)	Tax rate (percent)
10	0.00
20	0.00
30	2.85
40	6.89
50	9.31
75	12.54
100	14.16
200	16.58
500	18.03
1000	18.52

NOTE: These calculations apply for families who do not have interest and dividend income. The great majority of low-income families have only wage, salary, pension, or proprietorship income and no interest or dividend income. A small number of households, primarily retired, would pay higher consumption taxes than in this table because they do not enjoy the full benefit of the exemption unless they have wages, salaries, and pensions above the exemption limit.

In thinking about the fairness of the flat tax, I believe that we should concentrate on this table. Precision about the amount of tax paid today under the income tax by consumption category is difficult, but I do not think it is very different from this table.

Housing. The flat tax gives first-year write-off, in effect, to owner-occupied housing. It brings the service flow of housing under the tax where the flow escapes taxation under current income tax. It achieves neutrality between rented

117

and owner-occupied housing both with respect to investment decisions and with respect to families' rent-buy decisions.

To see this point, consider first the treatment of rented housing under the flat tax. The contractor and the contractor's suppliers pay the flat tax when they build a house, and that tax, as Eisner points out, is embodied in the price the landlord pays for the house. But upon purchase of the house, the landlord receives a first-year write-off that exactly offsets the tax built into the price of the house. So far, no net taxation. Then the landlord pays the tax on the rental receipts from the house. That amount is the only net tax, and it is a tax on the consumption of the house's services. Rented housing is thus taxed on the strict consumption tax principle. Now if the purchaser of the same house will be living in it, the same tax is embodied in the purchase price. There is no explicit first-year write-off or explicit taxation of the service flow from the house. The net tax paid is just the tax built into the price of the house. Because the price of the house equals the present discounted value of the future service flow, the tax paid by the homeowner is the same as the tax paid by the landlord. There is neutrality between renting and owning. The neutrality would be a little clearer if we allowed the homeowner first-year write-off, on the one hand, and then collected a tax on the service value of the house, on the other hand, but those two provisions would just offset each other. Collecting the tax once from the contractor and omitting the homeowner from the process are much simpler.

Eisner is right that the elimination of the mortgage interest deduction may be a negative influence on housing. Whether the fact that one can deduct interest on borrowing secured by a house has much effect on the value of housing or the demand for it is an unresolved question. After all, one can also deduct interest on borrowing secured by stocks or bonds, but no one has suggested that such borrowing affects the value of stocks and bonds.

The neutrality achieved by the flat tax may be going too far. Housing is taxed by state and local governments through property taxes. The combined effect of neutral federal taxation and state property taxation may indeed tilt against housing. So a logical modification of the flat tax might be to offer some offset to the flat tax based on the amount of property tax paid. Retaining deductibility of property taxes would be a possibility and would cushion whatever shock the removal of interest deductions might cause. These are elite issues, since about two-thirds of taxpayers do not itemize deductions under the current income tax.

Human Capital. Eisner observes that the flat tax does not have an explicit provision for first-year write-off of investment in human capital, just as the current income tax does not permit depreciation of human capital. The bulk of human capital investments are written off implicitly, however, under both the current income tax and the flat tax. When a teenager chooses not to work but rather to go to school, or when any worker accepts a lower wage in return for skills acquired on the job, there is an implicit write-off. The accumulation of human capital is treated on the consumption tax principle.

Eisner is right that the bias against cash investments in human capital is retained and worsened in the flat tax. Some economists have argued for the partial retention of deduction of state and local taxes to reflect their educational content. I see this issue as part of the much bigger question of the role of the government in providing education. I believe it should be considered not as part of general tax reform but rather as part of the reform of public education. Replacement of government-operated school systems by support of privately operated schools through vouchers seems the way to go. The role of the federal government in a voucher plan could easily be adjusted to give the equivalent of tax write-offs.

119

Intangible Capital. Eisner observes that investment in intangible capital is an important part of total capital accumulation in the U.S. economy. Under both the current tax and the flat tax, all business investment in intangible capital receives first-year write-off. It is treated strictly by the consumption tax principle, with no bias toward hardware investment. Similarly, investment of all kinds by state and local governments is treated neutrally. Here the demonstration of neutrality is exactly the same as for housing. When a local government builds a bridge or a school or trains its police force better, it pays the flat tax built into the prices it pays for those products. There is no write-off, but there is also no taxation of the future service flow. A business making the same investment would enjoy a write-off, but it would pay a tax on the earnings from the investment in the future. These offset exactly. Eisner's claims that the flat tax is biased against intangibles or against public investment are thus incorrect.

Eisner concludes that a broad tax that taxes all income exactly once is a good idea. Just as he would entertain the flat tax if given a choice only between it and the current tax, I would choose his proposal over the current tax. But his easy concession that it would be acceptable for the top bracket under his unitary income tax to be 46 percent was startling. How many trillions of dollars, over future decades, would the nation lose by the distraction of high-income successful people that would surely accompany that high rate?

Index

About the Authors

DICK ARMEY, majority leader of the House of Representatives of the U.S. Congress, was a principal architect of the Republican "Contract with America," supervising the drafting of the ten contract bills. He is known for his budget-cutting efforts, including advocacy of 1988 base-closure legislation and a 1990 coalition opposing outdated farm programs. He is a former chairman of the University of North Texas Economics Department.

CHRISTOPHER DEMUTH is the president of the American Enterprise Institute. Before coming to AEI in 1986, he was the managing director of Lexecon, Inc., an economics consulting firm. Previously he was an administrator for regulatory affairs at the Office of Management and Budget, executive director of the Task Force on Regulatory Relief in the Reagan administration, a member of the faculty of the Kennedy School of Government at Harvard University, and an attorney with Sidley & Austin. His articles on government regulation and other subjects have appeared in *The Public Interest, Harvard Law Review, Yale Journal on Regulation, Wall Street Journal,* and elsewhere.

ROBERT EISNER is the William R. Kenan Professor Emeritus at Northwestern University. He is a past president of the American Economic Association and a fellow of the American Academy of Arts and Sciences and of the Econometric Society. Mr. Eisner has published extensively in leading professional journals and in the *Wall Street Journal, New York Times, Newsday,* and *Chicago Tribune.* As a member of the

125

Los Angeles Times Board of Advisers, he writes periodic essays on the economy for its Sunday business section. Mr. Eisner's latest book is *The Misunderstood Economy: What Counts and How to Count It.* Among his other books are *How Real Is the Federal Deficit?, The Total Incomes System of Accounts,* and *Factors in Business Investment.*

ROBERT E. HALL, a senior fellow at the Hoover Institution and professor in the Department of Economics of Stanford University, is engaged in research on inflation, unemployment, taxation, and monetary policy. Mr. Hall was a professor of economics at the Massachusetts Institute of Technology and an assistant professor at the University of California at Berkeley. He is a fellow of the Econometric Society and of the American Academy of Arts and Sciences and is the director of the research program on economic fluctuations of the National Bureau of Economic Research.

ALVIN RABUSHKA is a senior fellow at the Hoover Institution at Stanford University, where he specializes in taxation, constitutional limitations on taxing and spending, and economic development, with special attention to East and Southeast Asia and Israel. Before coming to the Hoover Institution in 1976, he taught at the University of Rochester and the University of Hong Kong. He is the author or coauthor of numerous books on race, ethnicity, aging, taxation, state and local government finances, the economics of Hong Kong, Taiwan, Korea, and Singapore, and Israel's economy. His books and articles on the flat tax—published in scholarly journals and in the *Wall Street Journal, New York Times,* and *Fortune*—provided the intellectual foundation for several flat tax bills that were introduced in Congress during the 1980s.

HERBERT STEIN, a senior fellow at the American Enterprise Institute, was a member of the President's Council of Economic Advisers from 1969 to 1971 and was chairman from 1972 to 1974. He is the A. Willis Robertson Professor of

Economics Emeritus at the University of Virginia. In addition, Mr. Stein is a member of the Board of Contributors of the *Wall Street Journal.* Among his recent books are *The Fiscal Revolution in America* (AEI, 2d rev. ed. 1996); *The New Illustrated Guide to the American Economy,* with Murray Foss (AEI, 1995); *On the Other Hand...Essays on Economics, Economists, and Politics* (AEI, 1995); *Presidential Economics: The Making of Economic Policy from Roosevelt to Clinton* (AEI, rev. ed. 1994); and *Washington Bedtime Stories* (1986).